SS: Hell On The Eastern Front

The Waffen-SS War In Russia 1941-1945

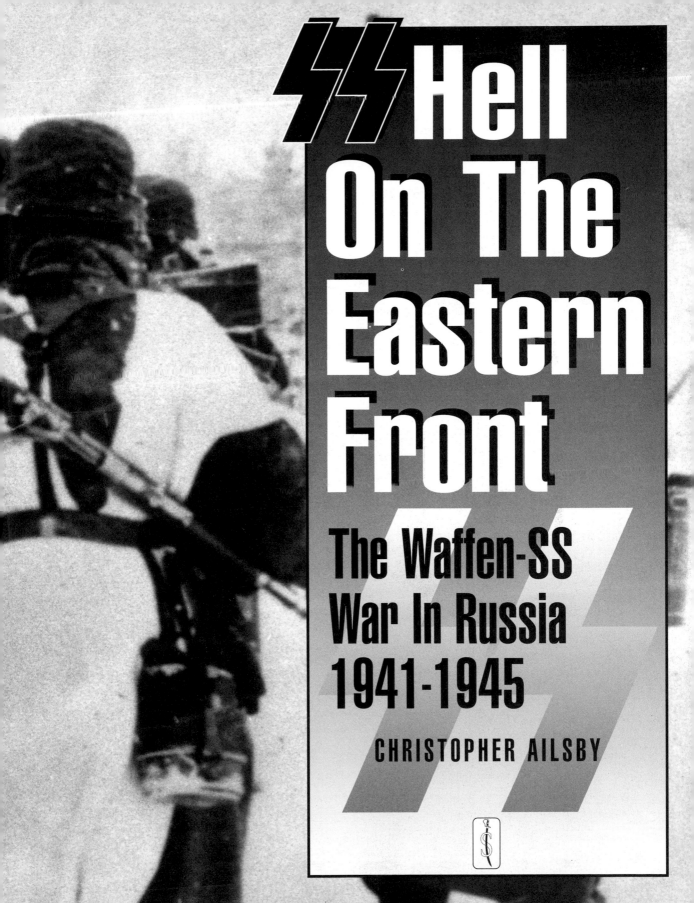

SS Hell On The Eastern Front

The Waffen-SS War In Russia 1941-1945

CHRISTOPHER AILSBY

British Library Cataloguing in Publication Data:
A catalogue record for this book is available
from the British Library

ISBN 1-86227-031-7

First published in the UK in 1998 by
Spellmount Limited
The Old Rectory
Staplehurst
Kent TN12 0AZ

1 3 5 7 9 8 6 4 2

Editorial and design: Brown Packaging Books Ltd
Bradley's Close, 74-77 White Lion Street,
London N1 9PF

Editor: Judith Millidge
Design: WDA
Picture Research: Christopher Ailsby and Ken Botham

Printed in Italy

Picture credits
All photographs Christopher Ailsby Historical Archives except:
Novosti Photo Library: 108-109, 130-131
TRH Pictures: 2-3, 13, 14, 60-61, 76-77, 94, 98-99, 115, 138-139, 142-143,
160-161, 167
TRH Pictures via Espadon: 112-113, 148-149

Previous pages: Frozen grenadiers of the **Der Führer** *Regiment,*
Das Reich *Division, during Operation 'Typhoon', the attack on*
Moscow, in the winter of 1941.

To Philippa

CONTENTS

THE IDEOLOGICAL WAR

Few troops were more ideologically motivated than the men of the Waffen-SS, especially those who first fought in Russia. To understand their fanatical dedication to SS principles, one has to examine the unit's humble beginnings, and the development of the organisation, in particular its rapid growth and the ideological indoctrination received at the hands of Theodor Eicke and his colleagues.

In the early days of Nazism, Hitler was surrounded by the unwieldy Sturmabteilung (SA), mainly unemployed ex-soldiers who frequented Munich beer halls and were recruited by Ernst Röhm, friend of Hitler, to protect Nazi speakers. The SA bodyguards grew in number, and acted under Röhm's orders rather than Hitler's. Hitler realised that a more dedicated élite personal guard was necessary; not large, but consisting of men of proven calibre, Nordic blood and good character. With an unequivocal allegiance to Hitler, they would act as his bodyguard, protecting both him and important members of the Nazi Party, while they travelled the breadth of Germany furthering its cause.

In March 1923 the embryo SS consisted of just two men, Josef Berchtold and Julius

Left: Adolf Hitler, Chancellor of Germany, inspects an honour guard of the Leibstandarte in Germany in the late 1930s. To his right is Reichsführer-SS Heinrich Himmler.

Left: Members of the Stosstruppe Adolf Hitler, the forerunner of the SS. Formed in May 1923, it was commanded by Josef Berchtold. His task was to protect Hitler at all times and serve him unswervingly. The unit was involved in the abortive Munich Putsch of November 1923, in which Hitler made a farcical attempt to take over Bavaria.

Schreck, who called themselves the Stabswache , or 'staff guard'. Two months later a new unit was formed, the *Stosstruppe Adolf Hitler*, commanded by Berchtold. The *Stosstruppe* was involved in the disastrous Munich Putsch in November 1923, which ended in fiasco, with the arrest of the leaders, Hitler in prison and the Nazi Party banned.

Heinrich Himmler escaped prosecution and returned to Landshut, where he sold advertising space in the party newspaper, the *Völkischer Beobachter.* He found himself a local party official with command over the tiny SS in his district. Gregor Strasser was appointed Reich Propaganda Leader of the Nazi Party in September 1926, and Himmler accompanied him to party headquarters as his secretary.

In April 1925, Hitler ordered his chauffeur and personal bodyguard, Julius Schreck, to raise a new shock troop. A few weeks later it was named the Schutzstaffel, or 'Protection Squad'. The new SS was to be organised on a national basis: each major city was called upon to provide one leader and 10 of its best men, but by 1928 it had only 280 members. Himmler's organisational ability had not gone unnoticed, however, and he was appointed Deputy SS Leader and then Reichsführer, (National Leader) in January 1929, with the

rank of SS-Oberführer. He commanded approximately 1000 men, and though the SS was still a part of the SA, Himmler gradually began to separate the two formations.

The growth of the SS

Overwhelmed by the large number of applications from ex-Freikorps (private armies raised after World War I) and unemployed middle-class volunteers, he introduced biological criteria and the concept of racial purity into new recruitment plans. The army, which perceived Röhm and his SA as a rival took a favourable view of the SS as a force. This, combined with Himmler's organisational skills, resulted in the growth of the SS. By 1930 it numbered 2727 men; in June 1932, when the SA was banned, the SS had grown to 30,000 or approximately 10 per cent of the SA's strength.

In the early 1930s, the political situation in Germany began to degenerate and take on the guise of near civil war. The Socialists and the Communist Party fielded armed militia, to which the SA and SS replied with force. Some 10 SS men were killed and several hundred wounded during the violent street battles with the Rötfrontkämpferbund, or 'Red Front Fighters' Association'. With the crucial 1933 elections approaching, it suited the Nazi Party to create the illusion that the country was on the slippery slope to all-out anarchy, and that it held the key to the political problems that abounded. By 30 January 1933, when Hitler became Chancellor, the SS had secretly recruited 52,000 more members.

On 27 February 1933 the Reichstag was burned down. Rudolf Diels, head of what was to become the Gestapo, reported to Hitler that the alleged culprit, Marinus van der Lubbe, was in custody and that the fire was the work of a single demented pyromaniac. Hitler, however, blamed the Communists and burst out in fury: 'This is a cunning plot! Every Communist official must be shot. All Communist deputies must be hanged this very night.' Two days later Hitler issued a 'Decree for the protection of People and State', which gave police powers to the SA and SS. Some 25,000 SA and 15,000 SS men were issued with firearms and deployed as Hilfspolizei or 'auxiliary policemen'. Police presidents were able to take into protective custody anyone considered to be a political opponent in the broadest sense of the term. The Reichstag fire allowed Hitler to flex his political muscles. The party's left-wing protagonists began to be unceremoniously ushered into prisons and makeshift unofficial camps or 'wild man camps', so called due to the lack of supervision and the frightful stories of brutality which emerged from them.

A decree on 26 April 1933 established the Geheime Staats Polizeiamt (Gestapa), which was later renamed Geheime Staats Polizei (Gestapo), as a new department of the Prussian State Police affiliated with the Ministry of the Interior, to be headed by Diels. The Gestapo (and Diels) became targets for the ambitious Himmler, who was desperate to control it.

'Night of the Long Knives'

The SS was divided into two distinct groups: the Allgemeine-SS – 'General SS' – which fulfilled a police function and was basically part-time, and the newly emergent Bewaffnete-SS or 'Armed SS', which was military in appearance and full-time.

The turning point in the struggle for supremacy over the SA was the assassination of its chief, Ernst Röhm, on 30 June 1934. A decree on 26 July recognised the part the SS had played in the purging of the SA and promoted it to the status of an independent organisation within the Nazi Party. Himmler set

Right: A rare photograph of the first SS volunteers, taken in 1925. In April of that year, Hitler had ordered his chauffeur and personal bodyguard, Julius Schreck, to raise a new unit. It was called the Schutzstaffel – Protection Squad – and initially numbered eight men. What was to become the most infamous organisations in modern history was thus born.

Left. Under Himmler's guidance the SS became an élite in Nazi Germany, which, in his own words, 'hesitates not for a single instant, but executes unquestioningly any order coming from the Führer'.

about implementing his theories of a racially and ideologically élite force, devoting his life to the expansion of the SS and giving it many facets. Himmler concerned himself with perfecting a future German élite through the SS. Not only would they be of guaranteed Aryan stock, but would be encouraged to form the new race through the Lebensborn network of maternity homes. The SS entered its second phase of rapid expansion, and by the outbreak of World War II the Allgemeine SS numbered some 240,000 part-time members, who were kept in readiness in case of internal strife by a small regular staff. So many members of the Allgemeine-SS were called up for service in the armed forces or Waffen-SS, that many Allgemeine-SS units survived in name only.

Himmler's power spreads

Himmler became Polizeipräsident of Munich after Hitler became Chancellor in January 1933. This modest post enabled him to gradually gain control of the German police network, except in Prussia, where Göring was Minister of the Interior. But he finally achieved complete control in 1936. From the security point of view he took over the Gestapo, and made it a Europe-wide organisation. Himmler greatly admired Reinhard Heydrich's considerable organisational abilities, total ruthlessness, intense anti-Semitism and Nordic appearance. He realised that Heydrich's fear of being considered partly Jewish would be a means of controlling him. Through Heydrich and the Sicherheitsdienst (SD), the party's intelligence and security body, Himmler formed an intelligence service that covered both internal and external operations.

Heinrich Himmler's man of steel was SS-Obergruppenführer und General der Waffen-SS Theodor Eicke, who was to play a key role in the liquidation of Röhm and his supporters.

Having refused to shoot himself, Röhm was dispatched by Eicke in his cell at Stadelheim prison at midday on 1 July 1934. That summer most of the unofficial camps, or 'wild man camps', were closed. The remaining SA camps were removed from the jurisdiction of the civil authorities and taken over by the SS. The first full time SS Konzentrationslager, or concentration camp unit, was recruited from members of the Allgemeine-SS and was entirely under the overall command of the SS District South, who made it a depository for its unwanted personnel. The conditions that the guards lived under were little better than the inmates'. In June 1934 Eicke took command. He improved conditions, lifted the morale and discipline of his men and formulated service regulations for both guards and prisoners which remained virtually unchanged until the end of the war. In recognition, Himmler appointed him inspector of concentration camps and head of the SS-Totenkopfverbände in 1934.

The growth of the military SS

Within three hours of Hindenburg's death on 2 August 1934, Goebbels announced the fusing of the two roles of Chancellor and President. The only barrier between Hitler and unrestrained power had fallen, and he was now in the position to dictate and reward. In return for the services they had rendered on the 'Night of the Long Knives', the SS became an expanding state-sponsored paramilitary force and the army had to come to terms with this fact. The chiefs of the three branches of the Wehrmacht were officially advised on 24 September 1934 of the creation of the SS-Verfügungstruppe. It was to be made up of three regiments modelled on infantry regiments of the army, each to contain three battalions, a mortar company and a motorcycle company, as well as being supported by a signals battalion. It also provided for three officer cadet schools. The formation was to be under the command of the Reichsführer-SS, except in time of war, when it was to come under the control of the army.

Hitler decided that he needed a Praetorian Guard. The state protection provided by the

Reichswehr or police could not, in his eyes, be entirely replied upon. Without delay Hitler decreed that a new full-time armed SS unit would be formed, whose primary role would be exclusively to escort him wherever he was in Germany. 'Sepp' Dietrich, one of Hitler's closest associates, was entrusted with the formation of the unit. Hitler was later to describe Dietrich as 'unique, a man who is simultaneously cunning, energetic and brutal'.

Dietrich undertook the task with zeal, and by 17 March 1933 the embryo of a new headquarters guard named the SS Stabswache Berlin was founded. It comprised 120 hand-picked volunteers, some of whom were former members of the *Stosstruppe Adolf Hitler* and whose loyalty to the Führer was unswerving.

Below: Theodor Eicke, Inspector of Concentration Camps and later commander of the Totenkopf *Division. Tough, cruel and humourless, he indoctrinated his men with an unremitting hatred for everything non-Nazi.*

Two months later, the unit was reformed as the SS-Sonderkommando *Zossen*, and enlarged with three training companies. The terms of engagement for the unit were expanded, and it could now be employed for armed police and anti-terrorist activities as well as the guard duties it already undertook. There was another metamorphosis during the next months, when a further three companies were formed as the SS-Sonderkommando *Jüterbog*. A rally was held on 31 August 1933 to mark the Nazi accession to power. Known as the Parteitag des Siegers, or Victors' Party Rally, it was a fitting occasion for Hitler to formally recognise the *Adolf Hitler* SS-Standarte and to dedicate the SS-Standarten, or regiments. This was formed from SS-Sonderkommando *Zossen* and SS-Sonderkommando *Jüterbog*. 'Sepp' Dietrich received the banner with the name 'Adolf Hitler' on the box that surmounted it. The two sonderkommandos were granted the honour and right to wear the name 'Adolf Hitler' on a cuff band on the left arm. The new formation was named the *Leibstandarte SS Adolf Hitler*.

Hitler's bodyguard

The ceremonial consecration was formalised in front of the Feldherrnhalle on the occasion of the Commemoration of the Munich Putsch on 9 November 1933. Here the members of the *Leibstandarte* took a personal oath of allegiance to Hitler, dispelling any doubts that these men were anything but his personal cohort. Himmler theoretically had control over the unit, but in reality the ultimate director of its function was Hitler. Guard Commander 'Sepp' Dietrich assumed an independence within the SS organisation for the *Leibstandarte* that no other unit enjoyed, provoking Himmler's complaint that it was 'a complete law unto itself'.

The *Leibstandarte* was used in the Röhm Putsch, and was employed in the arrests, with the detainees being reposited in the Lichterfelde Barracks. It was also instrumental in many of the killings. The number of executions undertaken by *Leibstandarte* firing squads is unknown, but it is reported that there were some 40 executioners employed. The *Leibstandarte*'s 'first blooding' was over when the shooting finally ended on 2 July. For their loyalty and involvement, Hitler promised Dietrich that the *Leibstandarte* would become a fully equipped regiment. The *Leibstandarte* was further honoured in early October 1934 when it became fully motorised. At this time, the Reichswehr in the main was still horse-drawn, and this decision led to hushed whispers of discontent in military circles. The Political Readiness Detachments were to be reorganised into battalions and then amalgamated within the *Leibstandarte* under Himmler's orders of 14 December 1934. The *Leibstandarte* now consisted of a headquarters, three motorised infantry battalions, one motorcycle company, one motor company, one signals platoon, one armoured car platoon and one regimental band.

SS recruitment

How were the recruits selected and indoctrinated in the SS generally, and the SS-Totenkopfverbände and SS-Verfügungstruppe specifically? Young university educated men, products of the national Youth Movement, were encouraged to join the SS. Many were motivated purely by power and a fear of a return to the chaos and instability of the inflation years. Predominately lawyers and economists, these men tended to gravitate to the SD or the SS-Hauptampt, which later became the Wirtschafts-und-Verwaltungshauptampt. Some volunteered for the fledgling SS-Verfügungstruppe, though a large proportion of the SS-Verfügungstruppe's officer cadres were middle-class soldiers who transferred from the Reichswehr, the small army Germany was allowed under the terms of the Versailles Treaty.

The officer classes were initially more difficult to persuade. Men from this background were unimpressed by the undisciplined rabble which comprised 90 per cent of SS membership in the early days. Revamping the SS with a new image of class and respectability required discreet political overtures to certain highly respected members of the old German aristoc-

Above: Reinhard Tristan Eugen Heydrich, Himmler's deputy and probably the most ruthless individual in the Nazi Party after Hitler. During World War II he organised the Einsatzgruppen in the East.

racy. Several prominent members, including the Grand Duke of Mecklenburg and the Princes of Waldeck and Hess, responded favourably. 'Cleansing programmes' resulted in the expulsion of some 60,000 men between 1933 and 1935, purging the SS of outright criminals, homosexuals, alcoholics, the 'professionally unemployed' and anyone who could not prove his racial purity. Standards were tightened for admission: racial purity, physical fitness, height and the lack of a criminal record became prerequisites for acceptance. At this

Above: Students attending a lecture on Nazi ideology at the SS officer training school at Bad Tölz. The SS training schools were heavily influenced by the Inspector of the SS-Verfügungstruppe, the able Paul Hausser.

time, the *Leibstandarte* disbarred from its ranks men who had a single tooth filled. By 1938, 12 per cent of SS officers holding the rank of SS-Standartenführer or higher came from the military aristocracy.

Another group whose recruitment into the SS was actively encouraged by Himmler, with his quaint rustic ideals, was farmers' sons such as Walther Darré. He wrote a book in which he advanced his philosophy that the Germans were both farmers and warriors. He recognised no clear division between nobility and peasantry, believing that every free man was noble in essence, since he could bear arms. He felt that Nordism was on the wane in Germany, and he linked this with the decline among the peasants. He considered that it was fundamental to create a new nobility, composed not of individuals but of families. He thus intimately linked the concept of blood and earth. For him there was no racism without roots. The earth was not made solely to feed people, but also to provide them with physical and moral health. He summed up his ideas in a formula: 'The death of the peasant is the death of our people. It is not merely bread which grows in furrows; it is men also.' Darré considered Christianity to be an evil influence, which destroyed the original concept of Germanism. Himmler embodied these thoughts into SS ideology, and tried, but never succeeded, to make the SS a religious body. His anti-Christian policies deterred many men who would have volunteered and would have been found suitable. Under these conditions and the rigorous standards now employed, the supply of acceptable recruits began to dwindle.

Young blood for the SS

At the age of 18 a Hitlerjugend – Hitler Youth – could become an SS-Bewerber, or applicant. On the Reich's Party Day of the same year he was accepted as an SS-Anwärter (candidate) and given an SS identity card. After a short probationary period he took the oath of allegiance to Adolf Hitler. At the age of 19 or 20, depending on when his age group was called, he went into the Labour Service and then into the armed forces

He returned to the SS, still as a candidate, if he elected not to remain in the armed forces, as a regular or noncommissioned officer candidate after his two years' service. The candidate was given special philosophical training, the principles of the SS being thoroughly explained, in particular the marriage order and code of honour of the SS. Subject to fulfilling all the special requirements, the SS candidate was finally accepted as an SS man. At a special ceremony on 9 November after his return from the armed forces, he vowed that he and his relations would forever observe the basic laws of the SS. The newly ordained SS man was given the right to wear the SS dagger, and from that day forth it was his right and duty to defend his honour, according to the code of honour of the Black Corps. He remained in the Allgemeine-SS on the active list until he was 35 years of age, when, upon application, he was placed on the SS reserve list.

The SS-Totenkopfverbände

Pre-war there were different qualification standards for the SS-Totenkopfverbände recruits and those of the SS-Verfügungstruppe. To join the *Leibstandarte* or SS-Verfügungstruppe, a recruit had to be at least 1.8m (5ft 11in) and later 1.85m (6ft 0.5in) tall and between the ages of 17 and 22. For the SS-Totenkopfverbände the height restriction was only 1.7m (5ft 7.5in) which was later reduced to 1.54 m (5ft 6.7in) tall and the upper age limit was 26. Neither organisation insisted on educational qualifications, and before 1938 40 per cent of SS recruits had only received what could be termed primary school education. Insistence on being able to prove their Aryan descent, in good physical and mental condition and to have clean police records was crucial. Himmler boasted in 1937 that 'we still choose only 15 out of every 100 candidates who present themselves'. Inevitably, standards had to be lowered to allow Himmler to continue expanding his empire. Gradually the religious standards, and those pertaining to height and physical fitness, were eroded, together with the all-important racial criteria. Service in the SS-Totenkopfverbände for noncommissioned officers and men was 12 years. Since this duty did not count as military service, Hitler ordered that volunteers be chosen from among those 'who, as a rule, have served their compulsory military duty in the army'. Most of the men recruited for the SS-Totenkopfverbände before the issue of the Führer Decree were youngsters aged between 17 and 19, and this practice did not altogether cease after 1938.

Theodor Eicke aimed to create a hatred for the churches as enemies of National Socialism by initiating a vehement anti-religious campaign in the SS-Totenkopfverbände, and many individuals who clung to their beliefs were victimised mercilessly. SS-Totenkopfverbände

personnel were under intense pressure to renounce their religious affiliations, and a large number had officially renounced Christianity by late 1936. Eicke's efforts were often rewarded, by a legacy of unbridgeable rifts between parents and their sons. Political fanaticism, élitism and camaraderie were Eicke's key doctrines.

Eicke viewed the SS-Totenkopfverbände as an élite within the élite structure of the SS. This concept grew from the fact that the most dangerous political enemies of the state were incarcerated in the concentration camps and Hitler had given sole responsibility for guarding and running the camps to the SS-Totenkopfverbände. Eicke repeatedly pressed home his principles in orders, circulars and memoranda. The whole of the SS-Totenkopfverbände training was based on élitism, toughness and comradeship, together with a regime of ruthless discipline. The slightest infractions of SS rules brought harsh and often brutal punishment. Each month was split

Below: Felix Steiner, the progenitor of Waffen-SS tactics. A World War I veteran, he was instrumental in creating SS soldiers who were very fit, highly motivated and trained in the tenets of mobile warfare.

Left: SS-Totenkopf recruits relax in the heady days just before the outbreak of World War II. By this time the formations of the armed SS had superb élan, and their officers had been taught to lead by example, which often resulted in their high casualties during the war. This was all part of the ethos of the SS, a closed community with its rules and loyalties.

into three weeks of training, followed by one week of guard duty within the concentration camp. The training, both political and military, was designed to shape the attitude and colour the outlook of the SS-Totenkopfverbände man. Participation in camp guard duty gave him exposure to the prisoners and conditions in the camps. Eicke felt that this experience would underpin the lessons learned during his training, strengthening the resolve that the prisoners were inferior but implacable enemies of the German state. Eicke's fanaticism knew no bounds; the SS had to wage an unending struggle against these enemies. The SS-Totenkopfverbände's behaviour suggests he created an atmosphere conducive to indoctrinated political fanaticism, which gave rise to the excesses perpetrated later during the war.

Political training was divided into three broad areas. The first dealt with the history of the Nazi Party, and included an examination of the party programme. The second involved the history and racial beliefs of the SS, with special emphasis placed upon the SS-Totenkopfverbände. The third and most important part required a careful analysis of the enemies of National Socialism. In order of importance

these were: the Jews, Freemasonry, Bolshevism and the Churches.

Theodor Eicke was appointed Inspector of Concentration Camps and head of the SS-Totenkopfverbände by Himmler in 1934. The inspectorate was established at Oranienburg, near Berlin, and the SS-Totenkopfverbände was enlarged and reorganised into five numbered sturmbanne, or battalions: I *Oberbayern*, II *Elbe*, III *Sachsen*, IV *Ostfriesland* and V *Thüringen*. In 1937 the five battalions were again reorganised, this time into three standarten which carried the designations *Oberbayern*, *Brandenburg*, and *Thüringen*. They were stationed in Dachau, Oranienburg and Frankenberg respectively. A few months later, Standarte *Thüringen* was transferred from Frankenberg to the Buchenwald concentration camp in Weimar. After the Austrian Anschluss a fourth regiment bearing the name Ostmark was established at Linz, later providing the guards for Mauthausen camp. From 1 April 1938, the organisation of the SS-Totenkopfverbände was fixed at: four standarten of three sturmbanne with three infantry companies comprising 148 men, one machine-gun company comprising 150 men, and medical, transport and communications units. By the end of 1938 Eicke's men had all received some basic military training. When World War II broke out he formed a division from the Totenkopf units, undergoing military training at Obermünsigen Würtemberg during the winter of 1939.

On 16 March 1935, Hitler announced to the German parliament that, in direct contravention to the Treaty of Versailles, he had reintroduced military conscription and officially established the SS-Verfügungstruppe. The intention was always that the SS-Verfügungstruppe would benefit from the highest possible standards of training available. Two highly regarded former army officers, Paul Hausser and Felix Steiner, were recruited for this purpose. Both were ultimately to become among the finest field commanders in the Waffen-SS. The SS-Hauptamt, or Main Office, established on 30 July 1935 was to organise all branches of the SS, and a special inspectorate of the SS-Verfügungstruppe was created on 1 October 1936 to supervise administration and military training. The new inspectorate had the objective of moulding the mainly ill-trained and far-flung units of the SS-Verfügungstruppe into an efficient fighting force.

Paul Hausser

SS-Oberstgruppenführer und Generaloberst der Waffen-SS Paul Hausser, who was to become known affectionately as 'Papa' Hausser to his men, was chosen as inspector of the SS-Verfügungstruppe, although he had only just been appointed inspector of the SS-Junkerschule (officer schools) at Bad Tölz and Brunswick. Once these two SS officer training schools had been established, he began attracting increasing numbers of former police officials and Reichswehr NCOs into the fledgling SS-Verfügungstruppe. Hausser readily accept-

Right: SS-Verfügungstruppe personnel on exercise 'somewhere in Germany'. By the time World War II broke out, the SS contained soldiers who were both fanatical and disdainful of death.

ed the responsibility for the organisation and training of the SS-Verfügungstruppe, which enabled him to formulate the directives and codes of practice it used. Few men had the same leadership qualities as Paul Hausser, and under his guidance the inspectorate fused the SS-Verfügungstruppe into a formidable organisation. Hausser remained inspector until the outbreak of World War II, when he took command of the *Das Reich* Division.

Felix Steiner

Felix Steiner was the luminary when it came to the actual training programme of the SS-Verfügungstruppe. He was 16 years Hausser's junior, with a charismatic personality. In 1935 he joined the SS-Verfügungstruppe and helped to develop the III Battalion of the SS-Standarte *Deutschland*, stationed in Munich, and the SS training camp at Dachau. He was promoted to command that standarte in 1936, instituting rigorous training schedules in application of his motto 'sweat saves blood'. In comparison to the staid and traditional army training, with its emphasis on 'square bashing', Steiner's ideas were revolutionary. He believed strongly in the creation of élite, highly mobile groups whose training put the emphasis on individual responsibility and military teamwork, rather than mindless obedience. He was diametrically opposed to the massed ranks of cannon fodder which still characterised most tactical thinking

at the time. His ideas had been formulated and refined during World War I when he served as commander of a machine-gun company, witnessing the formation of 'battle groups' which had greatly impressed him. They were made up of selected men, withdrawn from the trenches and formed into ad hoc assault groups. Specially trained for close-quarter fighting, usually carried out at night, they wreaked havoc in their trench raids, employing individual weapons such as knuckle dusters, cluster grenades and entrenching tools sharpened like razors. The customary notification of an impending attack, signalled by an artillery barrage, was often dispensed with, heightening the enemy's fear and surprise as a result.

SS training

As their value became recognised, Steiner's reforms gradually filtered through the SS-Verfügungstruppe hierarchy. Along with his 'battle group' ideology, he promoted a very strict physical programme conjoined with a regime of cleanliness (even to ludicrous extremes). He structured recruits' days with a rigorous hour's PT beginning at 0600 hours, with a pause afterwards for breakfast of porridge and mineral water. This was followed by intensive weapons training, target practice and unarmed combat sessions. The day was broken by a hearty lunch, then resumed with a comparatively short but intensive drill session. The afternoon was then punctuated by a stint of scrubbing, cleaning, scouring and polishing, rounded off with a run or a couple of hours on the sports field. His men spent more time on the athletics fields and in cross-country running than on the parade ground, and developed outstanding standards of fitness and endurance as a result, enabling them to perform such feats as running 3km (1.87 miles) in full kit in 20 minutes, achievements which could not be matched by either army recruits or even members of the *Leibstandarte*. The training programme was interrupted three times a week by ideological lectures: in the classroom the recruits had to sit up straight with their hands on the table.

One recruit in three failed basic training the first time round. Successful candidates took the SS oath at a passing-out parade separately from members of the other SS branches, at 2200 hours during the annual 9 November celebrations. These occasions have been described as a 'uniquely holy event on which the venerated cadre of the survivors of the Munich Putsch silently re-enacted their march through the crowd-lined streets of the Bavarian capital in a bombastic travesty of the Passion Play'. The finale was the torch-lit oath-taking ceremony for candidates of the SS-Verfügungstruppe, which took place in Hitler's presence before the Feldherrnhalle and the 16 smoking obelisks, each of which bore the name of the first fallen Party Faithful. The oath was a major ingredient in the SS mystique, binding each successful candidate in unswerving personal loyalty to Hitler. During the ceremony a voice intoned the 16 names, and after each one a thousand voices chanted 'Hier'.

The SS brotherhood

The candidate now had to spend a year in one of the SS infantry or cavalry schools, before returning to Munich to swear another oath binding himself to obey Himmler's marriage laws. This was an attempt to replace the Christian rites of marriage, christening and death. Marriages no longer took place in churches but in the open under a lime tree, or in an SS building decorated with life runes, fir twigs and sunflowers. Proof of Aryan ancestry was required to protect racial and physical purity. The recruit became a fully fledged SS man; officers of SS-Untersturmführer rank and above were given the SS dagger.

To be eligible for a commission in the SS-Verfügungstruppe, officer cadets had to have served for a minimum of two years in the ranks, which initially meant in the Reichswehr. Officers enlisted for 25 years, NCOs for 12 and privates for four, with basic training being the same for all groups. Officers had to undertake an intensive combat course, which included tests of courage such as having to dig a foxhole in front of an advancing tank. More significant were live firing exercises with machine guns, mortars and artillery.

One innovation introduced by Eicke and emulated by Steiner was designed to break down the rigid divisions between ranks which existed in the army. Officers and NCOs were encouraged to talk and mix with their men to get to know them as individuals. They competed in teams against each other on the sports field. Off duty they addressed each other as 'kamerad', rather than by rank.

Consequences of an ideology

On 17 August 1938, Hitler defined the *raison d'être* of the SS-Verfügungstruppe as being an armed force at his personal disposal, not a part of the armed or police forces. Therefore, it was able to be trained by the Reichsführer-SS in Nazi theories of race, and also to be manned by volunteers who had completed their time in the Reich Labour Service. The Führer's decree also stated that, in wartime, elements of the Totenkopfverbände would reinforce the SS-Verfügungstruppe. If mobilised, it was to be used firstly by the commander-in-chief of the army, making it subject only to military law and order, but still remaining a branch of the Nazi Party. Second, in an emergency within Germany, the SS-Verfügungstruppe would be under Hitler's control through Himmler. From these provisions emerged the first four of what were to become known in 1940 as the Waffen-SS divisions: the *Leibstandarte SS Adolf Hitler, Das Reich, Totenkopf* and *SS-Polizei,* plus the nucleus of a fifth, *Wiking*.

The consequence of their training was to dehumanise the troops. Ideological indoctrination convinced them that the Russians and other eastern Europeans were Untermenschen, or subhuman, who had no place in the National Socialist world. The Waffen-SS links with the Einsatzgruppen (Special Action Squads) was only a step away for units such as the SS-Totenkopfverbände in particular, whose training engendered a blind faith in the orders and ideology they received. All these factors would come together during the Waffen-SS's crusade in the East: the war against Russia.

Above: A pre-war SS-Totenkopf recruit, one of thousands of SS soldiers who believed that a war against the Soviet Union was the fulfilment of a dream: the beginning of the final battle against Bolshevism and Jewry.

FIRST BLOOD

Hitler did not regard the Nazi-Soviet pact of 1939 as a permanent feature of German strategic planning, a fact he never concealed from his generals. He advised his commanders in November 1939 that 'we can oppose Russia only when we are free in the West.' Russia 'is not dangerous' for the moment, he assured them. The victory in the West gave him the freedom of action he required to look eastwards. Britain was the only country unsubjugated, though militarily he chose to ignore or marginalise this fact.

The decision to attack the Soviet Union was a monumental one, equalled only by its rapidity. The failure to knock Britain out in a single stroke, combined with the temptation, the power and the sense of occasion, gave this Herculean step a structure and reality all of its own. Years of brooding and moments of intoxication thus fused fiercely into what General Warlimont subsequently called 'the ghastly development'. War with the Soviet Union was perhaps less baffling if viewed not as strategic or military rationality in the normal sense, but simply as Hitler's own brand of it.

Führer Directive No 21 was given on 18 December 1940, setting out the objectives of the campaign, planned to be launched in May the following year. This Directive stated:

'The bulk of the Russian Army stationed in western Russia will be destroyed by daring

Left: Grim-faced Waffen-SS soldiers aboard Krupp lorries towing 3.7cm PAK anti-tank guns during the early stages of 'Barbarossa'. The tracked vehicle is a StuG III

Above: As 'Barbarossa' unfolded, the Waffen-SS began to display those qualities it would bring to the Eastern Front: ferocity in attack, steadfastness in defence, and a fanatical pursuit of the ideological struggle.

operations led by deeply penetrating armoured spearheads. Russian forces still capable of giving battle will be prevented from withdrawing into the depths of Russia. The enemy will then be energetically pursued and a line will be reached from which the Russian Air Force can no longer attack German territory. The final objective of the operation is to erect a barrier against Asiatic Russia on the general line Volga-Archangel. The last surviving industrial areas of Russia in the Urals can then, if necessary, be eliminated by the Luftwaffe.'

The battles in the Soviet Union heralded spectacular victories, but also ushered in brutality of unimaginable depths, with neither side giving or receiving quarter. The crusade was now launched under the codename 'Barbarossa', taken from one of the heroes of German history, Emperor Frederic Barbarossa, who marched with his knights at the close of the twelfth century against the infidel in the Holy Land. The Waffen-SS, the Third Reich's military and ideological élite, were to engage in a new quasi-religious kind of war based on a clash of ideologies. The war in the East was promoted as a Wagnerian struggle of the *Herrenvolk*, or master race, against the *Untermenschen*, or sub-humans, to bring about the subjugation of those the party despised most: the Jews, Slavs and Bolsheviks.

The weakened Red Army

The Soviet armed forces had been decimated by Stalin's purges (named after the most prominent officer executed, Marshal Mikhail Tukhachedsky). Between 1937 and 1939 Stalin carried out the systematic destruction of the Soviet High Command, the primary motive being to secure his position as absolute ruler of the Soviet Union. Few events had more effect on the Soviet Red Army of 1941: three out of five marshals of the Soviet Union, 11 deputy commissars of defence, 13 out of 15 army commanders, and all the military district commanders of May 1937, as well as the leading members of the naval and air force commands, were shot or disappeared without trace. The same fate was suffered by the political apparatus which was supposed to advise the professional soldiers. During those two fearful years some 35,000 officers were either dismissed imprisoned or executed altogether. This purge damaged the ability of the Soviet Red Army to resist the German invasion when it came.

The Tukhachedsky affair had supposedly been manipulated by Heydrich, aided by SS-Gruppenführer Dr Hermann Behrends and SS-Sturmbannführer Alfred Naujocks. The information gained helped colour the timing and content of Directive 21. However, Stalin's infamous secret police, the NKVD, had achieved what the German military command and Heydrich's secret service could never have done: remove the most effective commanders the Red Army possessed.

The Soviet Red Army, totally paralysed logistically and operationally by the loss of some of its most able men, had pitted against it 11 German armies, four of them panzer and three air fleets. On paper the odds appeared to be uneven, with the Soviet Red Army fielding 230 divisions totalling some 12 million men supported by 20,000 tanks and 8000 aircraft, against approximately three million German soldiers accompanied by 3330 tanks and 2770 aircraft. Crucially, however, the advance of the Wehrmacht was obstructed by only about 130 Soviet divisions.

The Waffen-SS units were deployed among the various Army commands. Field Marshal Gerd von Rundstedt, commanding Army Group South, was allocated the *Leibstandarte SS Adolf Hitler*, and the *Wiking* Division, which were with General Edwald von Kleist's 1st Panzer Group. Army Group South comprised five panzer divisions, three to four motorised, 21-22 infantry, six mountain and three security divisions, along with 14-15 Romanian, two Hungarian and two Italian divisions. It was an impressive force.

Das Reich was allotted to General Heinz Guderian's 2nd Panzer Group and formed part of Army Group Centre, which comprised nine panzer divisions, five motorised and 31-35 infantry divisions, as well as two to three security divisions, a cavalry division and the *Grossdeutschland* Regiment under Field Marshal Fedor von Bock.

The weakest of the army groups, Army Group North, with only three panzer divisions, three motorised, and about 20 infantry divisions, was commanded by Field Marshal Ritter von Leeb; it was also assigned the *Totenkopf* Division as part of General Erich Höppner's 4th Panzer Group. The *SS-Polizei* Division was part of Army Group North's reserves, while SS-Kampfgruppe *Nordland* and SS Infantry Regiment 9 were deployed as part of the Norway Mountain Corps under the command of Colonel-General von Falkenhorst, and were committed to the far northern sector of the front in Finland.

Army Group South was allocated the initial task of cutting off all the Soviet armies west of the River Dnieper. The capture of Kiev,

Right: The initial phase of the war in Russia witnessed colossal Russian losses. In the air, for example, over 3000 aircraft were destroyed, and on the ground the Red Army lost some 89 divisions. The Nazi war machine seemed unstoppable, and in the ideological vanguard was the Waffen-SS, imbued with a hatred of the 'sub-human' foe. It seemed the supermen were going to have another easy victory in Russia.

Kharkov and the Crimea were the territorial objectives, before pushing on to the River Volga and Stalingrad. This city was of incalculable psychological significance; once taken it left the way clear to the all-important Caucasian oil fields. In what proved to be an over-ambitious plan, a force of some 46 divisions was to drive east, comprising the 6th, 11th and 17th Armies with the 1st Panzer Group. The *Leibstandarte* Division was assigned to XIV Corps of the 1st Panzer Group.

The 1st Panzer Group had the objective of breaking through the Russian lines south of Kowel and cutting off Soviet Red Army units to the southwest, restraining them until the infantry could eliminate them. They had to advance over 480km (300 miles) across difficult terrain. Hard metalled roads were not a common feature of the Russian landscape, thus speed was of the essence, as the packed dirt roads would be transformed into deep quagmires once the autumn rains started.

The Russians made full use of the natural obstacles of the Rivers Pruth, San, Bug and Dnieper, and deployed their lines of defences opposing Army Group South. Opposing it was a force of approximately 69 infantry, 11 cavalry and 28 armoured divisions under the command of General Kirponos and then Marshal Budyenni.

On the morning of 22 June 1941 at 0315 hours, what was to be hailed as the greatest continuous land battle history had ever witnessed erupted. The sudden flashes of thousands of artillery pieces seared the pale dawn, heralding the onset of Operation 'Barbarossa'. In this clash of Titans, the Wehrmacht was to wreak havoc upon the Soviet Red Army.

The Leibstandarte's war

With the exception of the *SS-Polizei* Division, within the first few days of the campaign all the Waffen-SS formations under army command were in action (the *SS-Polizei* Division followed suit in early August). Russian troops bypassed during the main advance were dealt with by two brigades of Himmler's Kommandostab RFSS, SS Infantry Brigade 1 and the SS Cavalry Brigade, which were deployed immediately behind the front.

Left: Russian rolling stock carrying armaments and supplies after being hit by a Luftwaffe attack. A key part of the Blitzkrieg was the prevention of the movement of enemy supplies and troop reinforcements. The complete air superiority of the Luftwaffe during the early stages of 'Barbarossa' greatly facilitated the advance of army and Waffen-SS units on the ground, and hindered Soviet force deployments.

On 27 June the *Leibstandarte SS Adolf Hitler* was committed to battle, leaving its assembly area and joining the 1st Panzer Group reserves. It finally went into combat on 1 July, when it crossed the River Vistula at a point southwest of the town of Zamosc. The German pincers had extended deep into Soviet territory by this time, and General von Mackensen's III Panzer Corps had been cut off near Rovno. The *Leibstandarte* was allotted the first major task of the eastern campaign, re-establishing contact with General von Mackensen's III Panzer Corps, and was soon engaging Soviet tanks. While pushing through a densely wooded area two Soviet tanks attached themselves to a German column, mis-taking it for a retreating Soviet unit. The column came to a brief halt just outside Klevan as night began to fall. The Soviet tank crews realised their awful error and broke away, speeding off into the night.

Klevan was quickly taken, and the advance moved on relentlessly. A few kilometres to the east of the town the forward elements of the

Above: Infantry of the **Das Reich** *Division engage Red Army troops in July 1941. The division was part of Field Marshal Fedor von Bock's Army Group Centre. After heavy fighting in August, it was temporarily rested.*

Leibstandarte Division's reconnaissance bat-talion found an empty, blood-soaked ambu-lance beside an abandoned German howitzer. A few hundred metres away they discovered the corpses of several German soldiers, their bodies mutilated and their hands bound with barbed wire. Pronouncing that the Russians 'must be slaughtered ruthlessly', the Waffen-SS replied to the atrocity in like manner – a fore-taste of horrors to come.

Such rapid progress was made by the armoured units attached to III Panzer Corps that great gaps began to open up between the widely dispersed German formations. The Soviets spotted these weakness and attempted to exploit them, attacking out of the Pripet Marshes to the north. The Soviets' primary tar-get was the so-called Rollbahn, the main

in the encirclement of enemy forces around Uman. Committed at the height of the battle for the seizure of the enemy positions at Archangelsk, it took the city and the high ground to the south with incomparable dash. In a spirit of devoted brotherhood of arms, the *Leibstandarte SS Adolf Hitler* intervened, on its own initiative, in the desperate situation which had developed for the 16th Infantry Division on its left flank, routing the enemy and destroying many tanks. Today, with the battle of annihilation around Uman concluded, I wish to recognise and express my special gratitude to the *Leibstandarte SS Adolf Hitler* for their exemplary efforts and incomparable bravery.'

The *Wiking* Division, led by the *Westland* Regiment, moved forward on 29 June 1941 from its start point on the northern wing of Army Group South and advanced decisively through Soviet-occupied Poland. At Lemberg on 30 June, spearhead units encountered the Soviet 32nd Infantry Division. Considerable pressure was placed on the Waffen-SS elements by the numerically superior Soviet forces, and had to withstand repeated attempts to force them back. With the arrival of armour from the division's reconnaissance battalion,

the balance finally swung in the Germans' favour, and they repulsed the Soviet counterattacks. The commander of the *Westland* Regiment, SS-Standartenführer Hilmar Wackerle, was fatally wounded by a single shot fired by a lone Soviet straggler while driving in his command car. His death was a great loss to the regiment. Lead units from the *Wiking* Division forced a crossing of the River Slucz at Husyantin, and together with other Waffen-SS troops were soon in the thick of the fighting on part of the Stalin Line defences. They met particularly strong Soviet forces, who counterattacked immediately. For a while the outlook for the Germans looked bleak. The fighting raged back and forth until the army's 1st Mountain Division arrived on the scene and relieved the beleaguered force. On 8 July the *Wiking* Division became engulfed in a torrential downpour while driving towards Kozmin, reducing the division's speed to snail's pace as

Below: A brief pause before the next assault. In Russia in 1941 the Waffen-SS was driven by an unshakeable belief in their Führer and the inevitable victory of Germany. Annoyingly, though, the Russians refused to give in.

the muddy roads were now no better than a quagmire. The divisional HQ at Toratscha was all but overrun, with the *Germania* and *Nordland* Regiments being engaged in bitter fighting. The *Westland* Regiment continued its push eastwards on foot, undertaking a four-day forced march through heavily wooded terrain to the River Ross. The *Wiking* Division had to pick its way gingerly through vast quantities of abandoned Soviet war materials and vehicles which littered the area. Control of the division at this point was taken over temporarily by III Panzer Corps, while the *Westland* Regiment was diverted south to Talnze to assist in closing the Uman Pocket.

Elements from the *Wiking* Division served from 7–16 August alongside the Luftwaffe's elite *Hermann Goring* Regiment, which was fighting to secure the northern flank of the 1st Panzer Group around Korsun and Schandorovka. To help contain heavy Soviet attacks, a battle group was also dispatched to Dnepropetrovsk from the *Westland* Regiment.

Blood bath at Zaselye

The 1st Panzer Group moved on when the Uman Pocket surrendered, renewing its advance in the direction of Bobry. The town fell on 9 August, when the Soviet defences crumbled and were overrun. Mainly cavalry units, the Soviets were no match for the Waffen-SS troops. The *Leibstandarte* Division moved on to Zaselye, which was quickly taken, although the Soviets immediately mounted a counterattack. Grimly holding on to its positions, the *Leibstandarte* fought for a week with the Soviets, who, with equal determination, tried to force them out. The attacks finally ceased on 17 August, with enemy losses totalling some 1000 men either taken prisoner, killed or wounded.

The *Leibstandarte*'s next objective was the large industrial city of Cherson, the first time the Waffen-SS infantry would be forced to storm a sizeable city in Russia. Cherson was defended by Soviet naval infantry who contested every street. Bitter house-to-house fighting inflicted heavy casualties on both sides. Soviet

Above: Kurt Meyer – 'Panzer-Meyer' – who as the leader of the Leibstandarte *Division's reconnaissance detachment bluffed his way out of a Soviet encirclement during the early part of Operation 'Barbarossa'.*

units showed the same degree of fanaticism and fearlessness in the defence of their homeland as the Waffen-SS displayed in the attack. After three days of fierce fighting the *Leibstandarte* took the city on 20 August, and earned a few precious days of rest and reorganisation in corps reserve. Then the division crossed the River Dnieper and struck out again across the barren steppe.

To the north, German units had established a small bridgehead over the River Dnieper at Dnepropetrovsk. This area had been home to a Soviet artillery school, and the entire district had been expertly plotted by its cadets. The Soviets had little difficulty in pinpointing German targets with accuracy and bringing

Above: 'Barbarossa' netted hundreds of thousands of Russian prisoners. These were a target for reprisals for atrocities committed against German prisoners, though some senior Waffen-SS leaders tried to prevent this.

The *Totenkopf* Division smashed its way into the Stalin Line on 6 July, and found the defensive network was particularly extensive in its sector. Heavy losses were sustained by the division, but it still forced its way through, establishing a bridgehead over the River Velikaya by nightfall. Fierce artillery fire rained down on the soldiers of the *Totenkopf* Division, and Eicke's command car hit a mine and he himself was wounded.

On 12 July the *Totenkopf* Division moved as part of the group reserve to Porkhov. A few days of welcome rest was all that was forthcoming, as LVI Panzer Corps had encountered

trouble to the northeast of Porkhov, so the *Totenkopf's* troops were sent back into action in support on 17 July. LVI Panzer Corps' flanks had again come under attack from the Red Army, and so Eicke's command was sent to fend them off. The *Totenkopf* Division was retained by LVI Panzer Corps, relieving the 8th Panzer Division, which went into reserve.

On 21 July the *Totenkopf* Division's advance began once again, moving through the dark forests and swamps of the region to the west of Lake Ilmen. The Soviets had withdrawn to a new defence position known as the Luga Line which ran along the Mshaga and Luga rivers. From 8 August the Soviets began a morale-sapping campaign, initiating counterattacks as soon as night fell. Rest in any form was all but impossible, as the *Totenkopf's* troops had to use all of their efforts during the day to force the determined defenders back. A battle of attrition was underway. Soviet losses could apparently be made good without delay, while the Germans were unable to replace fallen troops. Partisans, who were already operating behind the German lines, had infiltrated the *Totenkopf* Division's rear areas. They had managed to tap into the field telephone lines, and from intercepted conversations were able to glean where the division's weak points were located, and planned their strategy of attacks accordingly. To add to their misery, the *Totenkopf's* soldiers were mistakenly strafed by Luftwaffe aircraft.

Fighting without end

While the Soviet 34th Army was smashing into the German flanks in mid-August, a Nazi counterattack force was formed by combining the 3rd Motorised Division and the *Totenkopf* Division. The two German divisions surreptitiously worked their way around to the flank, and with devastating effect crashed into the unsuspecting Soviets. The 34th Army's shattered remnants were rounded up, along with massive amounts of equipment and vehicles. Numerous Soviet prisoners were taken, with over 1000 prisoners being snatched by the *Totenkopf's* military police troop alone. With no less than eight Soviet divisions destroyed, this had been an important victory for the Third Reich on the Eastern Front, though the attacking German units were significantly weakened by heavy overall losses.

On 22 August, the advance resumed as the *Totenkopf* Division crossed the Polist River and pushed eastwards towards the Rivers Lovat and Pola. For several days the drive continued almost unhindered, with prisoners being rounded up in considerable numbers. However, this situation did not last, as the retreating Soviets had dug in and were waiting for the *Totenkopf* Division to reach the Lovat. The Luftwaffe had switched its efforts temporarily to other areas, giving the Soviets the advantage of considerable air support. Attempts by the *Totenkopf* Division to force its way across the river failed. Powerful Soviet counterattacks forced the Germans to withdraw from the shelter of the woods near the river, giving cover to Soviet ground forces. In order to oust the Soviets from their well prepared positions, the *Totenkopf* Division renewed its attack on 26 August, suffering considerable casualties in the process – the highest recorded casualty rate in the corps at this time. The skies over the Lovat once again became the Luftwaffe's domain on 27 August, and it swiftly drove off the Soviet fighters and fighter-bombers.

Mud bogs down the Totenkopf

The *Totenkopf* Division's advance continued, with its reconnaissance battalion reaching the Pola River at Vasilyevschina just as the rains came. Almost immediately the division's vehicles were bogged down in the mud. The Soviets hit the *Totenkopf* Division with determined assaults, which it then spent two days desperately beating off. But all the time the advance was being slowed.

Right: A motorcycle team of the Totenkopf *Division in northern Russia in August 1941. The division had started the campaign with 18,754 men; by the middle of July 1702 officers and men had been killed or wounded.*

LVI Panzer Corps demanded that the *Totenkopf* Division press home its advance and cross the River Pola. These orders were received on 30 August by SS-Brigadeführer und Generalmajor der Waffen-SS Georg Keppler, temporarily commanding the battered *Totenkopf* Division while Eicke was recuperating. Seeing that his new command was in no fit state to attack such a well defended line, Keppler appealed to von Manstein, who agreed that the attack should be postponed for a few days. The Soviet attacks continued unabated, however, so there was to be no respite for the *Totenkopf* Division.

On 5 September the advance continued, but the Soviets had planted booby traps and peppered the *Totenkopf* Division's route with mines to slow its progress. Facing considerably stiffening resistance and ferocious Soviet counterattacks, the *Totenkopf* Division was once more forced onto the defensive by 12 September. It became clear that 'Barbarossa' would not defeat the Red Army. As the weather deteriorated, the Waffen-SS braced itself for its first winter in Russia.

THE FIRST WINTER

The German war machine that had smashed over the Soviet Union's borders and steam-rollered its way into her heartland during June 1941 had run out of steam by early December. The winter of 1941-42 was a hard time for the Germans in Russia. With the onset of colder weather the muddy roads began to firm up, and for a few weeks the German units were far more mobile. All this changed when winter proper set in.

On 10 October the *Wiking* Division was transferred from III Panzer Corps to XIV Panzer Corps. It advanced along the Melitopol-to-Stalino railway line towards Woroowacha in order to overtake fleeing Soviet units and cut them off. Progress was slowed dramatically by torrential rain which, once again, turned the roads into seas of mud. For more than a fortnight the rain fell relentlessly, allowing the Russians time to reassemble their scattered units and regroup. The *Leibstandarte* Division reached Taganrog on 11 October after driving eastwards aggressively for almost 400km (250 miles) over inhospitable terrain. It crossed the River Mius under heavy fire and began the assault on the city. After six days of continuous and heavy fighting, Taganrog was taken, and three days later Stalino succumbed. At the beginning of November 1941, the *Westland* Regiment was subjected to a savage barrage from Russian Katyusha rockets, which

Left: A Panzer Mk III and Waffen-SS soldiers during Operation 'Typhoon', the attack on Moscow. The first winter in Russia came as a shock to Wehrmacht and Waffen-SS alike.

Above: German troops in Rostov in November 1941. The capture of this communications centre was facilitated by the Leibstandarte's *panzergrenadier regiment, which seized a vital crossing over the River Don.*

had a shattering psychological effect on the Waffen-SS troops. A salvo of these projectiles landed among unprepared and unprotected infantry units, causing near panic.

When the majority of III Panzer Corps had caught up with the spearhead units the assault on Rostov began in mid-November. The capture of this essential communications link by the *Leibstandarte* Division was assured when it took a vital bridge over the River Don. Soviet engineers had mined the rail bridge with demolition charges, but it was still intact. Its imminent destruction, it appeared, was being considered by Soviet engineers. Seeing a locomotive standing by the bridge with a full head of steam, SS-Hauptsturmführer Springer, commanding the 3rd Company, SS-Panzergrenadier Regiment of the *Leibstandarte* Division, ordered his men to open fire with every weapon available, peppering the engine and releasing high-pressure steam from countless holes. The ensuing confusion provided the cover required to storm the bridge. Springer and his men went on to remove the demolition charges, ensuring the bridge's safety. The Soviets made frenzied but futile attempts to

dislodge the Waffen-SS troops, who held on tenaciously until reinforcements arrived. Springer was awarded the Knight's Cross of the Iron Cross on 12 January 1942 for this action.

During the Russian summer the German troops had endured scorching heat and choking dust, followed by torrential rain which made roads into impassable rivers of mud. But nature had stored up the worst horror of all: the full fury of the Russian winter. As the temperature began to plummet, the Germans were caught totally unprepared. No warm winter clothing was forthcoming, and they had to face the winter in summer uniforms. The mechanisms of their guns began to freeze, while vehicles had the oil in vehicle engines and sumps solidified. To thaw their vehicle engines, small fires had to be lit under them. But worse was the moisture which formed in the barrels of the machine guns and turned to ice, which split the barrels when they were fired.

Fresh objectives

The Soviets encountered fewer problems with the winter weather as they were better prepared and had an abundance of fur-lined winter clothing for their troops. To a great extent the Russian weather conditions determined the design of their vehicles, which were able to function when the cold weather rendered German vehicles all but useless.

Numerous senior army commanders had praised the *Leibstandarte* Division during this first phase of the war on the Eastern Front. They applauded both the offensive and defensive actions it had been involved in. Reichsführer-SS Heinrich Himmler was to receive an unsolicited letter from General von Mackensen in which he described the *Leibstandarte* Division as 'a real élite unit'.

The *Wiking* Division had bean allotted a new objective, Schachty, which lay farther to the north and had to be taken before winter finally closed in. The advance began on 5 November 1941, though a brief unexpected thaw turned the roads into swamps. In order to reach the road to Astoahowo the River Mius had to be crossed, and the Waffen-SS troops

Right: SS-Hauptsturmführer Heinrich Springer, who was awarded the Knight's Cross of the Iron Cross for leading the assault which captured the crossing over the Don in the face of heavy Russian fire.

struggled towards the higher ground in the direction of Perwomaisk-Oktjabrisk. The conditions became so bad that the troops were obliged to disembark. Instead of trucks carrying the troops, they had to push the trucks through the thick mud.

In an area between the 14th and 16th Panzer Divisions, the German forces had become very dangerously overstretched. They reached Oktjabrisk on 7 November, and the division sent a battle group south into the gap. Soviet units constantly probed the German positions during this period, attempting to find their weak spots. As a result, *Germania* seemed to be in almost constant combat, while the Waffen-SS troops doggedly attempted to thrust forward. Meanwhile, *Nordland* continued northeast, advancing towards Alexandrovka.

Soviet resistance was hardening. T-34 tanks were being deployed in ever-increasing numbers, and the German tank crews and anti-tank gunners were amazed by their tenacity. Until then, anything in their path had been swept aside. During the opening phase of the campaign they had encountered mainly obsolete light, thinly armoured vehicles such as the BT-5, which had easily succumbed to the Germans. The T-34 was a tank to be feared: fast, reliable, well armoured and with a powerful 76mm gun. Unless used at extremely close

ranges, the 3.7cm anti-tank guns which equipped most German units in 1941 proved ineffective against them.

XIV Panzer Corps was forced onto the defensive when it was subjected to a counter-attack by powerful Soviet forces on 23 November. The SS infantry were without adequate winter clothing, and with sub-zero temperatures many of them were soon crippled by frostbite. Conditions generally were worsening, and the Soviet 9th and 37th Armies gradually pushed the SS back to defensive positions on the River Tusloff. With inadequate troops to defend the many loops of the river the Germans were forced to withdraw, unable to hold their positions. They fell back west to the River Mius and dug in around Amurosjewka.

Left: Fierce fighting rages on the outskirts of Rostov in November 1941. When the city fell, some 10,000 Russian troops went into German captivity, most never to see their homeland again.

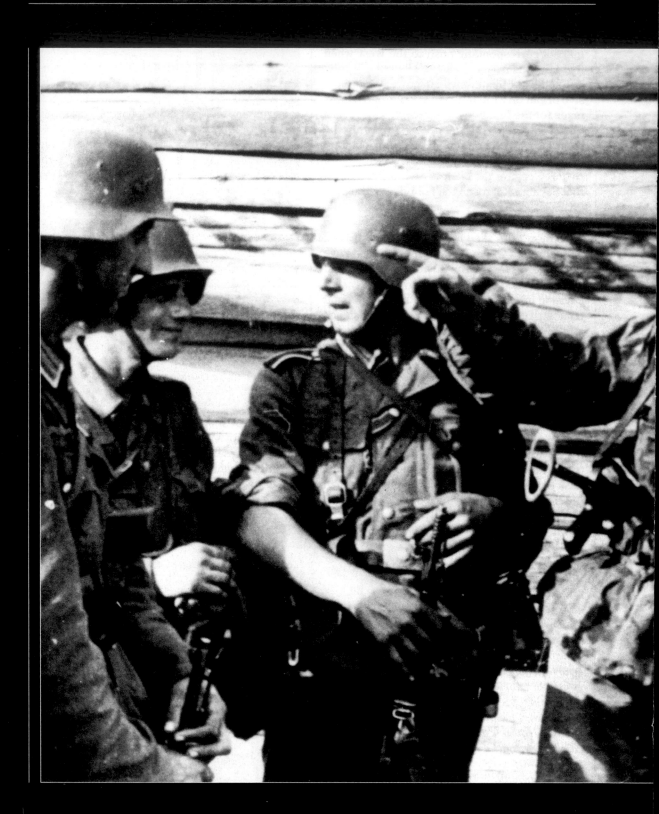

CHAPTER 4

A TIME OF TRIAL

The second year of the war on the Eastern Front, 1942, witnessed the growth and reorganisation of the Waffen-SS, seeing the birth of the powerful Waffen-SS panzer and panzergrenadier divisions. The Waffen-SS cadre divisions had been motorised by 1942, but as each had a panzer regiment they were panzer divisions in all but name. Before the end of 1942, however, they were redesignated SS-Panzergrenadier Divisionen, or armoured grenadier divisions. Their infantry regiments were soon after designated SS-Panzergrenadier Regimenter. The general background to the origins of the first divisions of the Waffen-SS and how they were created early in World War II from the full-time paramilitary formations of the existing SS gives an interesting insight into the development and expansion that now occurred.

The nucleus of the first of these divisions was the *Leibstandarte SS Adolf Hitler*, the Führer's personal bodyguard. The second was provided by the SS-Verfügungstruppe or SS-Special Purpose Troops, having at first passed through the transitional stages of being named SS-VT Division (mot.), SS-V-Division, SS-Division *Deutschland*, SS-Division *Reich*, finally being named *Das Reich*. The third was provided by elements of the SS-Totenkopferbände or SS-TV, the SS 'Death's Head' regiments, with the German police forming the fourth. The

Left: Wehrmacht and Waffen-SS in northern Russia, June 1942. Note the MP 40 submachine gun, complete with metal stock, slung over the shoulder of the SS grenadier.

TRIUMPH AND DESPAIR

Hitler flew into one of his uncontrollable rages when he learned that his order regarding Kharkov had been disregarded. When he regained some measure of composure, he demanded to be flown to Field Marshal von Manstein's Army Group South headquarters at Zaporozhye for an explanation.

In order to escape to German-held ground farther west, SS-Obergruppenführer Hausser and his troops had to go along the 'Kharkov Corridor' that had now contracted to little more than 1.6km (one mile) wide. The action was carried out in the nick of time.

Having freed this important strategic city from the Nazi hordes, the Soviets felt a great sense of achievement. However, their forces were exhausted both by the tenacity of the German defence, and by the immense loss of life, so their offensive faltered. Troops had to be replaced and the Soviet euphoria was soon tempered by these realities.

In grand manner, Hitler ordered that Kharkov must be retaken. The Soviets could easily be ejected and an immediate counterattack could, and should, be launched, he stated. The élite I SS Panzer Corps would very soon be

Left: Leibstandarte *soldiers on the edge of Kharkov in March 1943, just prior to the German retaking of the city – one of the Waffen-SS's greatest victories in Russia.*

reinforced by the arrival of the *Totenkopf* Division and could then undertake the task. Field Marshal von Manstein wanted to use I SS Panzer Corps for other purposes, however, deploying it as the upper claw in a large pincer movement, the objective being to encircle and isolate the Soviet armies who were moving towards the River Dnieper.

XLVIII Panzer Corps pushed towards the River Samara from its position east of Dnepropetrovsk with the task of securing bridgeheads across it. Once this was achieved its objective was to make itself ready for an attack into the area to the rear of the Soviet 6th Army, by striking northwards. This unexpected German push completely took the Soviet troops by surprise, and they retreated northwards in near panic. German morale soared, as the troops were pleased to be on the attack again. Vacating their positions around Poltava, the *Totenkopf* and *Das Reich* Divisions moved towards the southeast. In appalling conditions, the terrain covered with deep snow and shrouded in fog, they hammered the rear of the Soviet 6th Army.

Manstein's master stroke

The lower claw of the pincer would be formed by the army's 4th Panzer Army under the command of General Hermann Hoth. But Hitler would not be swayed from his primary objective of retaking Kharkov, and von Manstein perceived that it would be fruitless to attempt it. Just as von Manstein was about to bow to the inevitable, Hitler's plan was thwarted.

The fly in the ointment was the *Totenkopf* Division's inability to move off the main roads and travel across country, as an unexpected thaw had completely bogged it down. Thus delayed, the *Totenkopf* Division could not be employed in Hitler's plan. Until this time, progress had been excellent, but to improve on this Eicke decided that his heavy vehicles would travel faster over the frozen ground. The division picked up speed at first, but as the temperature unexpectedly rose the frozen soil thawed, and within a short time their axles were covered in deep mud. Eicke and his division were wallowing in this thick, treacle-like substance, making any progress at all virtually impossible.

Hitler now begrudgingly approved Field Marshal von Manstein's alternative plan, and the German counterattack began almost immediately. *Das Reich's* first objective as it drove west and southwest was Krasnograd. Its next target was Peretschepino, which was quickly taken. The division's morale was much improved when it received a personal message from Hitler on 20 February, in which he detailed their next objective.

On 22 February 1943, *Das Reich* punched towards Pavlograd supported by Luftwaffe Stuka ground-attack aircraft. Refitted with state-of-the-art weaponry and now fully motorised, the division fell upon Soviet cavalry units that lay in its path. Formidable fighters who used almost medieval tactics, the Russian Cossacks horrified the average German infantry troops. However, with no armoured cover at all, and only carrying *schashas*, the Cossack sabre, the Waffen-SS swept them aside like matchwood, inflicting horrendous losses upon them. The might of the Waffen-SS proved too much for Pavlograd, which succumbed on 24 February. The territorial gains achieved by the Germans were so fast that numerous 'friendly fire' actions occurred. This was graphically illustrated when elements of *Das Reich* came under the *Totenkopf's* panzer regiment guns, whose fire caused many Waffen-SS casualties.

After the *Totenkopf* and *Das Reich* Division joined forces, they swung to the northeast and drove parallel to the retreating line of Soviets, hammering the enemy's flanks. When the Soviet units became short of fuel, the Waffen-SS troops found that they simply abandoned their vehicles, all in full working order, forming long, immobile columns of tanks and trucks.

Right: Well-wrapped Waffen-SS grenadiers trudge through a Russian village towards Kharkov and victory, vindicating Hitler's belief in the military prowess of the newly created I SS Panzer Corps.

In the ensuing days, the demoralised Soviet forces endured what can only be described as slaughter. *SS-Totenkopf* Panzergrenadier Regiment 1, commanded by SS-Obersturm-bannführer Otto Baum and accompanied by men from the *Das Reich* Division, had been dispatched to block their escape route. This immensely strong SS unit wreaked havoc on the panic-stricken enemy, and the panzers were joined by dive-bombers of the Luftwaffe. They destroyed two complete Soviet armies, capturing or immobilising some 600 enemy tanks, of which the majority were the latest Soviet design, the T-34. The *Das Reich*'s panzer regiment was later able to employ a full tank detachment of recovered T-34s. A further 600 anti-tank guns and in excess of 400 artillery pieces was also added to this catalogue of success. The number of Soviet prisoners was not so impressive, however: approximately 9000 were captured and 23,000 killed. The reason being that Soviet troops abandoned their heavy equipment and made good their escape on foot, through gaps in the German lines.

The Germans also suffered considerable casualties. Possibly the most notable was the former concentration camp inspector SS-Obergruppenführer Theodor Eicke. This brutal man had won many enemies throughout his career, both within the SS itself and the army. His abrasive and uncouth manner endeared him to few in either service, but he was popular with the men of his division. He set an example by eating the meagre rations they were served and living in the same filthy, damp conditions in the field. The manner of his death was typical of that of many of his troops.

The death of Eicke

The divisional headquarters had temporarily lost contact with its panzer regiment on 26 February. Apprehensive at not being able to contact the regiment by radio, Eicke decided to investigate the situation personally. A Fieseler Storch scout plane was made ready and went on a reconnaissance mission. After a period of scouring the terrain, Eicke spotted elements of the regiment holed up in a small

village. He ordered the pilot to land, but the next village was still held by the Soviets, a fact Eicke had not observed. Landing between the two villages, the plane was caught in a hail of bullets, crashed, and was engulfed in an inferno of flames. The panzer regiment immediately attempted to rescue Eicke, but was beaten off. The following morning, the charred bodies of Eicke, his adjutant and pilot were eventually rescued with the loss of several lives by a specially formed assault group. His men were deeply saddened by the loss of their commander and he was given a Viking-style burial at a divisional cemetery near Orelka, Russia. His memory was further honoured when SS-Totenkopf Infantry Regiment 3 was named 'Theodor Eicke' and permitted to wear a cuff band with the former divisional commander's name embroidered on it. Later in the war this regiment was redesignated SS-Panzergrenadier Regiment 6.

Russian attempts to hold Kharkov

In order to block any German pushes towards Kharkov, the Soviet High Command, or STAVKA, deployed more troops into the sector, with the area south of the city receiving an armoured corps, despite the pressure its units were under. A trap had been set by the Germans and these fresh Soviet troops moved straight in to it.

The Red Army units were facing south, opposite the *Totenkopf* Division and *Das Reich*. Once Hausser had moved the *Leibstandarte* Division into their rear, a Soviet retreat was impossible. The *Leibstandarte* Division quickly established defensive positions as the *Totenkopf* and *Das Reich* Divisions levered the Soviets north towards them. The enemy was totally annihilated by *Leibstandarte* infantry, who had armoured support which was considerably strengthened by the new heavy battalion equipped with the mighty Tiger tank. With this last hurdle removed, the gates of Kharkov now lay open to the Germans.

I SS Panzer Corps and the 4th Panzer Army joined forces on 4 March and from their step-off point at Staroverovka to begin the assault

on the city. With the objective of forcing a bridgehead across the River Mscha, the *Leibstandarte* Division drove to Valki which was situated on it. The *Totenkopf* Division, which stood on the left flank of the *Leibstandarte* Division, had taken Stary Mertschyk then drove on to Olshany, which fell on 9 March. *Das Reich* was on the *Leibstandarte*'s right flank, but found that atrocious terrain slowed its progress, although its advance unit still reached the outskirts of Kharkov on 9 March. Peretdinaga and Polevaya were subsequently taken on the evening of 9 March by the *Leibstandarte*.

The original plan, promulgated by Hausser, was that Kharkov was to be taken by a three-pronged assault. The *Totenkopf* Division was to have attacked from the northwest. The north of the city was saved for the *Leibstandarte* Division, while *Das Reich* drove around to the north and attacked Smiyev down the eastern side. Scrapping this move, an attack on

Above: Fighting in Kharkov in March 1943. I SS Panzer Corps had spearheaded the operation to retake the city, prompting Hitler to remark: 'The SS Panzer Corps is worth 20 Italian divisions.'

Kharkov from the west became *Das Reich*'s new task. Defence was initially light when *Das Reich* penetrated the outskirts of the city, but stiffened dramatically thereafter.

To the north, pushing down the main Belgorod-Kharkov road, SS-Panzergrenadier Regiment 1, under the command of SS-Standartenführer Fritz Witt, smashed into Kharkov. On Witt's right flank was SS-Panzergrenadier Regiment 2, commanded by SS-Standartenführer Theodor 'Teddi' Wisch. The left flank was taken by SS-Obersturmbannführer Kurt Meyer, who was ordered to cut off the road from Kharkov to Liptsy, north of the city. 'Panzer-Meyer' decided that it was a better bet to travel through the woods, so he

ordered his reconnaissance battalion off the road and into the great forest, but his armoured vehicles found the new terrain difficult. Meyer began to have second thoughts when he discovered sled tracks and decided that following them might be a better option. The tracks soon narrowed, however, and the column was forced to halt several times to manhandle the vehicles, which were in danger of becoming stuck, through the obstacles. Meyer decided that he must catch up with SS-Obersturmführer Gerd Bremer, who commanded the forward element. Leaving all the navigational problems to his subordinates, he set off, finally finding Bremer and his men in a large clearing. The clearing sloped away, and at its foot stood a main road, on which Soviet Red Army soldiers were massed in their thousands, complete with tanks and artillery. With only a handful of light vehicles and a command of just over 20 men, Meyer knew that his force had to remain hidden.

Above: Elated with their victory at Kharkov, Hitler insisted that the 'SS gets the necessary personnel'. The **Leibstandarte, Das Reich** *and* **Totenkopf** *Divisions also got the latest heavy tank – the Tiger – for the Kursk Offensive.*

All he could do was cross his fingers, send back messages to warn the oncoming column so that they would know what lay before them, and await its arrival. The Germans then heard aircraft, a sound they knew heralded the arrival of Stuka dive-bombers. The aircraft bombed and strafed the Soviet column, which was scattered. Seizing this opportunity, Meyer ordered his minuscule force to attack immediately the lead tanks came into view. Fearing they had walked straight into a well-planned German ambush, the Soviets panicked. Some tried unsuccessfully to flee, while many others decided to put up their hands to surrender. Hundreds of prisoners fell into the Germans' hands, and Meyer's column, hoping to maximise the element of surprise, drove to Kharkov as fast as possible, leaving a handful of men to guard their prisoners.

They reached the city's northern outskirts without further incident and maintained a rapid progress until they came to the edge of the city, where Meyer called a halt at a disused brickworks. Meyer and his command retraced their steps to the earlier engagement battleground, where countless Soviet prisoners, who seemed relieved to be out of the conflict, were being supervised by a handful of grenadiers. The other members of Meyer's battalion arrived during the next few hours. The full force was regrouped by dawn the following day and with Kharkov their next port of call, their advance was resumed. Revisiting the brickworks, they destroyed or drove off all the nearby Soviet tanks located there. A shortage of fuel made further progress impossible, and Meyer gave the order to dig in on 11 March.

Meyer's unusual choice was a graveyard, and unbeknown to him the main escape route out of the city was situated alongside his force.

During the next few hours the Waffen-SS troops repulsed numerous Soviet attempts to overrun their positions. Meyer learned from the crew of a fuel tanker that had struggled through to his group that the Soviets had cut the road to the north of the city. His escape route was therefore blocked. However, the centre of the city had been penetrated by Fritz Witt's regiment, which had seized Red Square. Meyer had no choice other than to drive onwards into the city itself.

Caught by the impending German advance, the Soviet units in the city struggled fiercely to break out to the north. The *Das Reich* Division penetrated the city's western side, and on 12 March reached the main railway station at the heart of Kharkov, having overcome strong opposition. Meyer and his reconnaissance

Below: Though the Tigers and Panthers stole the limelight at Kursk, the older German tank designs, such as this Panzer III, also played their part in the greatest armoured clash in history, and were used by the Waffen-SS.

group in north Kharkov were relieved by SS-Sturmbannführer Peiper and his panzer-grenadier battalion. Together, they smashed a path to the east and southeastern sectors with the objective of flushing out what remained of the Soviet defenders. Now Kharkov was in German hands, Peiper and his units fixed Belgorod firmly in their sights and captured it on 18 March 1943, enabling the Waffen-SS to link up with the *Grossdeutschland* Division.

The victorious Waffen-SS

The *Totenkopf* panzers confronted Soviet units which had cut the Kharkov-Belgorod road and destroyed them. Their swing round the north of the city was continued southeast to Tshuguyev, where they captured the Donetz crossing. During the next few days the *Totenkopf* Division had to repulse Soviet units fleeing from Kharkov, as well as having to cope with counterattacks launched by fresh Soviet formations to the east. The Soviet High Command took cold comfort from all this effort, for during these actions the Soviet 25th Guards Rifle Division was annihilated.

After three days of fanatical close-quarter fighting in the city the Waffen-SS won Kharkov, but lost a great number of its men: over 11,500 killed. Hitler now perceived his political warriors in an even more invincible light. The Kharkov victory forged the reputation of the Waffen-SS as having fearless heroism in attack and steadfastness in defence. Hitler was convinced that the Waffen-SS could undertake the most dangerous and difficult missions with impunity, and during the remainder of the war he relied upon its divisions to fulfil the victories he desired and thought possible. The Waffen-SS, in return, tried to deliver what the Führer expected.

Once Kharkov had been retaken, the situation stabilised on the southern sector of the Eastern Front as the Germans set about consolidating their positions. However, it soon became apparent that the Red Army had established a huge salient between Kharkov and Orel in the north, extending into German territory and almost inviting attack. Hitler was transfixed by it, and soon preparations were under way to eradicate it. Once again the Waffen-SS was called upon to regain the German initiative on the Eastern Front. But the retaking of Kharkov had blinded Hitler to what was really happening: that despite his vaunted Waffen-SS he was losing the war in the East, a fact that would be confirmed at Kursk.

In the summer of 1943 one of the monumental clashes of World War II took place on the Eastern Front: the Battle of Kursk. Like the conflicts at Moscow and Stalingrad, it was terrible in its intensity and vast in scale. Armies of millions of men on each side were locked in a fierce and stubborn struggle which raged unabated for 15 days. The tank battles were the largest in the war, and in fact the greatest clash of armour in history.

Plans for the Kursk Offensive

As stated above, in mid-1943 the Eastern Front was overshadowed by a huge salient around the city of Kursk. Hitler, as ever, based his ideas on what he perceived as Nazi ideological thought. He saw that the Germans had to gain the initiative in the East, which would be achieved by liquidating this salient. He also believed that his flagging east European allies would receive a most welcome boost to their morale. Turkey, Germany's old World War I ally, had declared her neutrality, but this action could swing her into the war against the Allies. The German front would be dramatically reduced, as the bulge measured a mere 160km (100 miles) across its base. The military advantages were numerous: not only would it reduce the pressure on the number of men required to defend the line, it would also release a great number of troops from the Eastern Front to counter the expected Allied invasion of southern Europe. It would have the added advantage of destroying up to 15 Soviet armies if the offensive was successful. The German war effort would also be greatly enhanced by the countless numbers of Soviet prisoners who could be used as slave labour.

Field Marshal Erich von Manstein and General Heinz Guderian put forward a plan

suggesting that the Soviets be allowed to go onto the offensive and the Germans withdraw gradually, allowing the Soviets to over-extend themselves, as at Kharkov.

Hitler was unimpressed by the plans, despite the fact that they came from two of Germany's finest military brains. Hitler insisted that the offensive be planned and undertaken with all speed. It was to be codenamed Operation 'Zitadelle', or 'Citadel'. At one of the conferences in the Reich Chancellery, the Chief of Staff of OKW, Field Marshal Keitel said: 'We must attack on political grounds.' Germany's military and political leaders also assumed that successes in the East would rattle the very foundations of the Allied coalition, causing it to disintegrate under pressure from Soviet dissatisfaction at American and British delays in opening a second front. Hitler believed that 'the sooner a heavy new blow is struck at the Soviet Union, the sooner the coalition between East and West will fall apart'.

After the plan had been considered from all these angles at the highest level, Hitler issued

Above: The Waffen-SS just before the Kursk Offensive – confident, cocky and equipped with some of the best equipment available. II SS Panzer Corps was the spearhead of Germany's last great offensive in the East.

an order on 15 April 1943 for an offensive in the Kursk Salient. The order stated: 'This offensive is of decisive importance. It must end in swift and decisive success. On the axis of the main blow the better formations, the best weapons, the better commanders and a large amount of ammunition must be used. Every commander, every private soldier, must be indoctrinated with awareness that the decisive importance of this offensive victory at Kursk will be a beacon for the whole world.'

The main blows against the Soviet forces were to be struck from south of Orel by the 9th Army of Army Group Centre and from north of Kharkov by the 4th Panzer Army and Panzer Group *Kempf* from Army Group South. By striking in the general direction of Kursk, the German High Command reckoned to surround

Above: The lull before the storm. A German 10.5cm le FH 18/40 field gun waits for orders to pound Soviet positions in the Kursk Salient. The Germans deployed 10,000 artillery pieces to support the offensive.

and destroy the forces of the Central and Voronezh Fronts defending the salient, to straighten the frontline, and in the event of success to develop their offensive into the rear of the southwest front – plan 'Panther'. Nor did they exclude the possibility of a subsequent strike to the northeast, to outflank Moscow and come out behind the whole of the Soviet forces in the centre of the front.

Since such special importance was attached to the forthcoming battle, OKH reviewed and revised the 'Citadel' operational plan several times; Hitler stated more than once that 'there must be no failure'. Divisions which were to take part in the offensive were rested and made up to full strength in men and material. Particular attention was paid to the Soviet defensive system in the salient and to the terrain. Every square metre, according to General Mellenthin, was photographed from the air.

The German forces faced Soviet forces of massive and powerful might. General Rokossovsky commanded the Soviet Red Army on the Central Front, while General Vatutin commanded the Voronezh Front. Air Marshal Rudenko commanded the 2nd, and Air Marshal Krasovski the 16th Air Armies respectively, which were to supply airborne support. Eleven complete armies were positioned in the salient itself, while another massive force commanded by Colonel-General Konev was held in reserve on the Steppe Front. Colonel-General Goryunov's 5th Air Army provided reserve air support. The Soviets could call on over 1,300,000 men, 3300 tanks, 20,000 artillery field pieces and some 2000 aircraft – a force of unsurpassed magnitude.

In reply to this Herculean force stood one of Germany's greatest field marshals, Erich von Manstein, who commanded Army Group

South. This comprised Panzer Group *Kempf*, commanded by its namesake General Kempf, and was made up of XI Corps, commanded by General Raus and comprising the 106th and 320th Infantry Divisions; XLII Corps, commanded by General Mattenklott, comprising the 39th, 161st and 282nd Infantry Divisions; and finally III Panzer Corps, commanded by General Breith, comprising the 6th, 7th and 19th Panzer Divisions and 168th Infantry Division. The 4th Panzer Army, commanded by Colonel-General Hoth, was the other portion of Army Group South. It comprised II SS Panzer Corps, commanded by SS-Obergruppenführer Hausser and made up of 1st SS Panzer Division *Leibstandarte*, 2nd SS Panzer Division *Das Reich* and 3rd SS Panzer Division *Totenkopf*; XLVIII Panzer Corps, commanded by General von Knobelsdorf, was formed by the 3rd and 11th Panzer Divisions, 167th Infantry Division and the *Grossdeutschland* Panzergrenadier Division; finally there was LII Corps, led by General Ott and formed by the 57th, 255th and 332nd Infantry Divisions. General Dessloch's Air Fleet IV provided the air support.

Army Group Centre

Field Marshal Günther von Kluge was a traditional Prussian officer who showed considerable aptitude for his chosen profession. But he was also marked by a 'vacillating character and weak-minded opportunism'. His sharp mind recognised the monstrosity of the Nazi regime, but he also saw considerable personal and professional advantages in cooperating with it. He was one of the few German generals who had favoured the invasion of the Soviet Union. His command was Army Group Centre, whose forces consisted of Colonel-General Model's 9th Army, XLI Panzer Corps, commanded by General Zorn, XXIII Corps, commanded by General Freissner, and XLVII Panzer Corps, commanded by General Lemelsen. Colonel-General Ritter von Greim's Air Fleet VI was to provide air support.

The Germans fielded some 900,000 men, 2700 tanks and 10,000 artillery field pieces. Air cover would be supplied by approximately 2000 Luftwaffe aircraft. This, too, was a catalogue of awesome might. Tacticians might perceive these two opposing forces as reasonably matched, given the fact that the Germans had engaged and defeated a Soviet force eight times its size at Kharkov. The Waffen-SS would play a disproportionately large part in the campaign, considering Hausser's command formed under 10 per cent of the total German strength. Kharkov had been won using updated versions of the old Mk III and the newer Mk IV tanks, although a few of the more powerful Mk VI Tigers had also seen service. These tanks were used at the Battle of Kursk, and more Mk VI Tigers became available. The Germans' greatest hopes lay with the Mk V Panther medium tank. The clumsy Ferdinand assault guns were also employed.

Soviet preparations

Soviet detection of the German build-up was hardly an intelligence coup, given the preparations required for the massive offensive. The physical movement of equipment and men, combined with the dramatic increase in radio activity told all. General intelligence-gathering provided further proof, and the British passed on information gathered from the code-breaking activities at Bletchley Park.

The Soviet position, from Stalin's point of view, was that the Soviet Red Army should take the offensive. His generals in the field and the High Command, however, promulgated the idea to prepare first-class defensive systems; the German armies should then be encouraged to attack and be drawn into the salient. In attempting to smash through the Soviets' extensive defence obstacles, they would bleed themselves to death. Then would be the time to launch a savage counterattack. Stalin was persuaded by their point of view; his plan, of course, would have found favour in the eyes of von Manstein and Guderian.

Some 300,000 local civilians were employed by the Red Army to help in the preparation of the defences. Elaborate steps were taken to prevent a German breakthrough. The fronts were reinforced with large numbers of guns,

tanks and aircraft, the greatest concentration being made on the most likely axes of attack. Almost half the artillery regiments of Supreme Command Reserve allotted to the front were placed on the sector held by the 13th Army, for example, which covered the most vulnerable axis along the Orel-Kursk railway. The army was also given the 4th Breakthrough Artillery Corps, which had 484 guns, 216 mortars and 432 field rocket launchers. This provided an unprecedented concentration of artillery defence of about 155 guns and mortars of calibre exceeding 76mm, per 1.6km (one mile) of front – one and a half times the density established by the Germans for the coming offensive. As the Germans hoped to attain their objectives by massed use of tanks, the front commanders took special care over anti-tank defences, based on anti-tank strongpoints and

Above: Grenadiers of II SS Panzer Corps show a swastika flag to Luftwaffe aircraft to designate friendly areas during the opening of the Kursk Offensive. The corps fielded some 350 tanks for the assault.

areas, and systems of minefields. Artillery reserves were allocated and trained in good time, as were mobile obstacle detachments. The strongpoints, as a rule, were allocated between three to five guns each, up to five anti-tank rifles, and two to five mortars between a section, a platoon of sappers and a section of submachine-gunners. On the most important axes, the anti-tank strongpoints had up to 12 guns each. Anti-tank and anti-personnel obstacles were also widely employed.

The depth of defence of the Central and Voronezh Fronts on the axes of probable attack reached 152-176km (95-110 miles). Adding the defence line of the Steppe Front and the defence line along the River Don came to 256-288km (160-180 miles), and comprised eight defence belts and lines. To picture the scale of the work done in the preparatory period, on the Central Front sector more than 4960km (3100 miles) of trenches and communication lines were dug, enough to reach from Moscow to Irkutsk. On the same front the engineers laid about 400,000 mines and bombs, and the average density of minefields on the Central and Voronezh Front reached 2400 anti-tank and 2700 anti-personnel mines per 1.6km (one mile) of front, six times that of the defence of Moscow and four times that of Stalingrad.

The Soviets believed that the Germans would concentrate their maximum efforts on the northern part of the salient. But this was a mistake. A spearhead formed from the Waffen-SS's *Leibstandarte, Das Reich* and *Totenkopf* Divisions' armoured formations led the German offensive that was launched on the southern side of the salient. A massive artillery barrage began on the northern sector on 5 July at 0430 hours, launched by Army Group Centre with the intention of softening up the enemy positions. The Soviet defences did not suffer as badly as expected, and the assaulting Germans were surprised to encounter Red Army units ready and willing for action. The Soviets immediately responded with gun and heavy mortar fire. The anti-personnel mines that had been laid so liberally now wreaked havoc on the German troops who tried to conceal themselves in the tall grass. On the western flank the German push was beginning to bog down, and they advanced only a few kilometres by the end of the first day. The 20th Panzer Division and the 6th Infantry Division, situated

Below: Kursk yielded the usual crop of Russian prisoners, but the Red Army soldiery in general fought well and inflicted heavy losses on the Germans. The **Leibstandarte** *lost 97 killed on the first day.*

a little to the east, were having more success against the Soviet defences, where German armoured units penetrated about 8km (five miles) into the salient. However, the Soviet Air Force was able to mount effective air attacks, despite the Luftwaffe's air superiority over the area, and the Germans suffered heavy casualties in men and equipment.

The German armour suffered from the Soviet minefields, although Ferdinand tank destroyers and Tiger tanks played an important part in neutralising the Soviet T-34s.

In an unpleasant shock, the Germans realised that the Soviet defenders were responding with a tenacity and strength that they were not prepared for. Army Group Centre was greeted with a resistance that was far greater than anticipated, for the Soviet troops had concentrated in the north. During the whole offensive, the furthest penetration on the northern sector was only 16km (10 miles). The objective, Kursk, lay 80km (50 miles) from the frontline.

II SS Panzer Corps attacks

Prompted by intelligence gleaned from prisoners, over 600 Soviet guns delivered an artillery barrage in the south, as they believed that a German attack was looming. Along the front's entire length the German artillery opened fire with a ferocity unseen as yet. The weight of munitions used during this inferno surpassed the total used by the Germans during the Polish and French campaigns.

German radar detected the approach of Soviet aircraft when they targeted German air bases, so that the Luftwaffe intercepted them, and were more effective in the south than in the north.

The town of Oboyan was the first objective of Hoth's 4th Panzer Army, and initial progress was good. XLVIII Panzer Corps had the task of protecting the left flank of the assault. By the close of the first day the *Grossdeutschland* Division, in the company of the 3rd and 11th Panzer Divisions, was in the vicinity of Cherkasskoye and quickly overcame the first lines of defence around it. But this was at a

high cost: when 10 Panzer Brigade encountered an extensive Soviet minefield 36 of its new Panther tanks were destroyed.

In order to protect the right flank of the Germans' advance, Hoth decided to neutralise the Soviet reserves as a priority, rather than leaving them for later. He ordered an attack to be launched in the northeast after the Soviet defence lines had been penetrated. II SS Panzer Corps, commanded by Hausser, was given the mission of eliminating the Soviet reserves. II SS Panzer Corps was one of the strongest elements the German arsenal could unleash on the enemy. It had an enormous spearhead of armour which comprised 200 self-propelled guns and in the region of 350 tanks. An integral Tiger unit was attached to each of the SS divisions.

The SS engineers swept the first set of minefields dexterously aside, allowing Hausser's troops easy passage through them during their assault at 0400 hours on 5 July.

The Totenkopf *forges ahead*

The Panzerkeil, or 'armoured wedge', was deployed to cut through the Soviet defences, which it managed like a hot knife through butter. The point was made up of Tiger tanks, flanked by Panthers, which were only marginally lighter. Standard Mk IV and Mk III models with StuG III assault guns flanked the Panthers and formed the point of the German advance. By the end of the first day Hausser's men had penetrated 19km (12 miles) into the salient.

II SS Panzer Corps' right flank was guarded by the *Totenkopf* Division, and its objective was the Soviet 52nd Guards Division. After tenacious combat on both sides, the Soviets were overcome. The Soviet 69th Army's command post, which housed numerous high-ranking staff officers, was situated in the village of Yakovlevo, and all were captured by the close of the first day.

The division advanced rapidly, penetrating the salient by almost 32km (20 miles) and crossing the main Belgorod-Oboyan road by the end of the second day. Progress slowed, however, when Soviet resistance stiffened. The

following day the *Totenkopf* Division plodded on slowly but relentlessly, severing many important rail and road links, and plunging a further 16km (10 miles) into the salient. The Luftwaffe's ground-attack Stukas, which had 37mm anti-tank cannon fitted under each of their wings, rendered valuable assistance to the *Totenkopf* Division during this time.

At this point in the battle, the Soviet 6th Guards Army had been divided into two forces. It was clear that if the drive were to continue the *Totenkopf* Division would have to be deployed elsewhere. The mission of covering II SS Panzer Corps' flank was given to the army's 167th Infantry Division, and it spent most of 8 July waiting for replacements to arrive.

The Germans were to be subjected to a counterattack that was to be launched from a spot northeast of Belgorod. This was to be carried out by II Guards Tank Corps and had been ordered by General Vatutin. This powerful force was ordered to smash into the *Totenkopf* Division and II SS Panzer Corps' flanks. The

Above: A Waffen-SS sniper searches for targets in a Russian village during the Kursk Offensive. Mopping-up operations were an essential part of any large assault to ensure secure supply and communications lines.

Germans became aware of the move, however, and before the Soviets could reach the *Totenkopf* Division's position, they were subjected to a massed onslaught by bombers and fighter-bombers of the Luftwaffe that completely annihilated them.

More Soviet defence lines were attacked by the *Totenkopf* Division on 9 July, and the Soviet defences began to crumble within hours. The following day the SS reached the River Psel.

The extent of the advance was now causing deep concern to the Soviet commanders, who decided it was now time to commit the 5th Guards Tank Army and two tank brigades to crush the German spearhead. They were to be moved from northeast of Prokhorovka, where they were being held in reserve.

On 5 July the *Leibstandarte*, which was positioned to the south of the *Totenkopf* Division, pushed on, with progress, at first, being extremely good. The first line of the Soviet defences was penetrated, but gradually the division's advance was stifled by heightened Soviet resistance. It took stock of the situation but nothing was going to stand in the path of the *crème de la crème* of Germany's élite political warriors. These were the men of Hitler's bodyguard division, no less.

Heavy Waffen-SS losses

During the days that formed the overture to the battle of Kursk, the Waffen-SS divisions and the *Leibstandarte* in particular demonstrated many acts of heroism and leadership. But this was not without a monumental loss. On the first day of the offensive, the *Leibstandarte* suffered 522 wounded and 97 killed in action. This rose on the second day to 906 wounded and 181 killed, representing a 10 per cent casualty rate for the division in the space of 48 hours' combat. On the other hand, the Red Army was suffering casualty rates far in excess of those suffered by the Waffen-SS. Some units were, to all intents and purposes, virtually wiped out.

Although Russian losses were appalling, they were able to fill the gaps with replacements from what appeared to the Germans as a limitless manpower pool. The Germans did not have such great manpower resources to call on, and trained reserves were becoming scarce. German Army units became bogged down on the flanks of Hausser's II SS Panzer Corps, but in contrast the Waffen-SS's advance continued despite its losses. By the end of the third day another problem was emerging – tank losses were critical. Some 160 Panthers had been lost from the initial total of 200. However, the formidable Tiger tanks were knocking out

*Right: Tiger tanks of the **Das Reich** Division rumble forward at Kursk. Ironically, the slow-moving Tiger was more suited to defensive warfare, where from good positions it could wreak havoc with its 8.8cm gun.*

many Soviet tanks before the latter could close the range and use their guns against the massive armour that cloaked the Tiger. Mechanical teething troubles bedevilled the Panther, its newer companion, but it showed immense promise for the future. The Ferdinand had, through a design oversight, not been equipped with a machine-gun for close-quarter defence. This small but critical oversight had left this monster, larger than the Tiger, unbelievably defenceless in these situations. Once they had penetrated the Soviet positions, these mammoths became very vulnerable to the satchel charges and Molotov cocktails of the Soviet 'tank destruction' teams. Their crews were left with little else but their personal side arms to defend themselves.

Wittmann – tank ace

On 7 July the *Leibstandarte* began to push forward towards the towns of Teterevino and Oboyan. SS-Untersturmführer Michael Wittmann proved his worth, adding seven further tanks and 19 anti-tank guns of the Soviet 29th Anti-tank Brigade to his rocketing score. Wittmann and his Tiger crew had already knocked out eight enemy tanks on the first day of the offensive. He became known as the most famous tank killer of the war, achieving his first kills with an assault gun. It was not until early 1943 that he received his first Tiger tank on the Eastern Front. The secret of his success was patience, often waiting for his victim to come within very close range. By June 1944 he was accredited with 138 tanks and 132 vehicles destroyed. But it was the battles round Kursk that first brought him into the limelight, and by the end of the offensive he had destroyed 30 enemy tanks and 26 anti-tank guns.

Psyolknee was next in the sights of the Waffen-SS. Here, a powerful armoured counterattack was mounted when between 50 and 60 T-34s manoeuvred in an attempt to gain the rear of the SS-Panzer Regiment 1. Finding himself faced with this formidable destructive force, a 20-year-old Tiger tank commander, SS-Oberscharführer Franz Staudegger, engaged the enemy without a second thought.

Staudegger and his crew, labouring to fire and reload at a satanic speed, blew massive gaps in the enemy ranks with their tank's deadly 8.8cm cannon. On the battlefield he accounted for 22 T-34s destroyed, while the remaining T-34s beat a hasty retreat to avoid the attacks levelled at them by German troops equipped with Teller mines. Staudegger was immediately recommended for the Knight's Cross of the Iron Cross, which was confirmed on 10 July 1943. A veritable graveyard of T-34s had been established in the area around Teterevino, as some 90 tanks had been knocked out by the 2nd Battalion of Panzer Regiment 1, under the command of SS-Sturmbannführer Martin Gross, in the space of just three hours. SS panzergrenadier 'tank destroying' units accounted for a further 30 enemy tanks.

Das Reich, positioned on the right flank of the *Leibstandarte*, again met stiff resistance. Before the launch of the offensive, assault troops from the division had wormed their way into the enemy's first line of defences, which they were quickly able to immobilise. However, serious casualties were suffered by the division's second wave when they were caught in the Soviet barrage provoked by the initial German advance. The rain again played a major part, turning the ground into a quagmire. Not only did the panzergrenadiers have to struggle through this, but they were also without tank protection, as the rain-soaked ground had delayed their heavy support vehicles.

Das Reich *breaks through*

The village of Beresov was *Das Reich's* major objective on the first day of the offensive. The Luftwaffe's Stukas supported the division, which captured the village by rushing past and then swinging round and attacking the enemy in the rear. A ridge of high ground beyond the village was also taken as the division rattled on. Its objective achieved, it drove forward to exploit its success. Its momentum was only halted when it encountered the extensive belt of minefields at Bey and Beresov. The Soviet lines were breached the following day, despite the troops' struggle through the mud. *Das*

Reich's armour now flowed through the gap, and the main road to Lutscki also lay open.

The *Totenkopf* Division, leading II SS Panzer Corps, carried on driving northwards, and to the west of Prokhorovka the Soviet forces were cast aside. The 5th Guard Tank Army was positioned a little way to the east of the town. This, the main reserve of the Soviets, was preparing its own offensive, with the objective of bringing II SS Panzer Corps to a standstill. However, the Soviet preparations were rudely interrupted by the appearance of Hausser's command, which turned smartly eastwards with the *Totenkopf* Division taking the left flank, the *Leibstandarte* the centre and *Das Reich* the right flank.

The Soviets just managed to hold the Germans to the west of Prokhorovka, by launching desperate counterattacks against them. They also had to endure constant air attacks from the Luftwaffe, which was pulverising the defenders. The Soviet command faced a dilemma with regard to the German

Above: A Waffen-SS MG 34 machine-gun team searches for enemy aircraft during the Battle of Kursk. The weapon is mounted for the anti-aircraft role, while in the background is a downed Russian MiG-3 fighter.

advance. If they held back their counterattack to allow all their units to become fully deployed, the Germans would have time to acquire reinforcements from III Panzer Corps, which was driving northwards along Hausser's right flank. The tactical balance would move in the Germans' favour when this force arrived with its 300 or more tanks.

A Soviet decision to delay would invite disaster, so they implemented a two-part plan. A force of two mechanised brigades, a mechanised guards corps, an armoured brigade and a guards rifle division was dispatched with the objective of intercepting III Panzer Corps and halting it, or at least slowing its progress. The remaining force would immediately attack II SS Panzer Corps, meeting it square on.

All Soviet positions that could be located were subjected to an enormous Luftwaffe bombing raid when the German attack started once more on 12 July. The Panzerkeil was again used by the Waffen-SS divisions. To complete the softening-up process, a tremendous artillery barrage was laid down on the Soviet positions at the same time.

Carnage at Prokhorovka

With the advantage of the sun at their backs, which was to dazzle their enemies, the Soviets broke cover and at full speed drove straight at the amazed Germans as the German artillery barrage ceased. The experienced German gunners gave a good account of themselves and many Soviet tanks were knocked out. A considerable number reached the German lines, however, and battle commenced at virtually point-blank range. This favoured the Soviet T-34's lighter 76mm gun, and the effect of the smaller calibre was devastating. Tanks on both sides were blown apart by direct hits. Suicidal bravery was often demonstrated by the Soviet tank crews, who, once their ammunition was spent, deliberately rammed the enemy. A T-34 travelling at top speed, weighing 29.5 tonnes (30 tons), has a sobering effect on an enemy tank and its crew.

The *Totenkopf* Division, positioned on II SS Panzer Corps' left flank, was engaged by XXXI Guards Corps and XXIII Guards Corps, who halted the *Totenkopf*'s advance and forced it onto the defensive. II Guard Tank Corps provided stiff opposition to *Das Reich*, which found its weight too much to shake off.

The high point of the battle was reached by the afternoon, but the outcome hung by a thread and could have swung either way. The Soviet blocking force had achieved its objective and halted III Panzer Corps, which was battling to advance towards II SS Panzer Corps. This was a blow for Hausser.

In a desperate attempt to redress the situation and influence the result in their favour, the *Leibstandarte* regrouped. The very last vestiges of the Soviet reserves were now committed to the fray as the Soviets had successfully anticipated the Waffen-SS divisions' move. By nightfall, with both sides utterly exhausted by the fierce fighting that had raged all day, the battle was reduced to all but a handful of small individual skirmishes. Some 300 German tanks had been destroyed and many more had suffered major mechanical problems, effectively disabling them. The Soviets could recover their damaged tanks and repair or cannibalise them wherever possible. They took fearful casualties but were in command of the situation on the battlefield. Hitler officially decided to suspend Operation 'Citadel' on 13 July, although the fighting continued until 15 July. Nothing positive could come out of the battle, not even the smallest hint of limited success. Field Marshal von Manstein argued that the offensive could have some chance of limited success if it were relaunched with less ambitious objectives to continue the pressure on the Soviets. The final nail in the coffin for Operation 'Citadel' was Hitler's determination to withdraw the *Leibstandarte*, *Das Reich* and *Totenkopf* Divisions from the Eastern Front. The Allied invasion of Sicily, which had begun on 10 July 1943, preyed on Hitler's mind during the next three days, caused him to become increasingly concerned. The Italian Front could only be strengthened, in his opinion, by his élite Waffen-SS divisions. The soft underbelly of Europe was potentially where Germany's greatest danger lay. Hitler gravely reduced the strength of troops in the Kursk region to such a point that it was unlikely to withstand a Soviet counterattack. The offensive's territorial gains would all have to be sacrificed to the Soviets, which was the case by 23 July.

Kursk – the reckoning

The battle had inflicted resounding losses on both sides. The German losses were catastrophic in both men, which was estimated at around 100,000, and tanks. The Wehrmacht was never to recover from this disaster. The Eastern Front drained the German forces through attrition; the initiative had been lost and would never be regained. The Soviet catalogue was even more horrendous, though the

extent was concealed from the country until the collapse of the Communist regime in 1989. They suffered over 250,000 killed and 600,000 wounded, and 60 per cent of their entire tank strength was destroyed. But for them the battle marked the turning point of their war.

In Hitler's view, the Waffen-SS had once again proved without doubt its superiority, which he attributed to Nazi ideology. The army units on the flanks were thrown back or held their positions, but up to the last second of the battle his political warriors were advancing.

Before the Waffen-SS divisions could be transferred to the West they were transported for a short period of rest to an area near Kharkov. On 25 July, General Malinovsky ordered a counterattack against the German forces deployed in the Donetz Basin. The German positions along the Mius River were attacked and Field Marshal von Manstein's troops were overrun. On 30 July, the army's

Above: Waffen-SS grenadiers under fire at Kursk. By 12 July 1943, the German offensive had been halted. The Russians had suffered 50 per cent tank losses, but they had wrested the initiative in the East from the Germans.

16th and 23rd Panzer Divisions were moved south with the *Totenkopf* and *Das Reich* Divisions and committed to the conflict when they reached Stalino. The front was stabilised after three days of merciless butchery, and the Soviet push was halted.

The German situation was still very perilous, and they were soon to suffer two attacks delivered by three complete Soviet Fronts around Belgorod and in the direction of Orel. To cover Field Marshal von Manstein's forces left flank once more, the *Totenkopf* and *Das Reich* Divisions were hastily dispatched northwards. In the East, the writing was on the wall for the Third Reich.

CHAPTER 6

HIMMLER'S FOREIGN LEGIONS

It still seems incredible that thousands of men, whose countries had been overrun and conquered by the Nazis, should volunteer for service with the SS, the very force which had delivered a vicious and crushing blow to their compatriots. Why did these men accept military service with the German armed forces, let alone the SS with all its connotations? And why did the SS recruit them, and having done so, trust them in battle? This chapter examines the foreign units which fought in the Waffen-SS on the Eastern Front, units which on the whole made a valuable contribution to the Third Reich's war in Russia.

The origin of the foreign volunteer legions lay in Heinrich Himmler's quest for a pan-German Europe. Himmler had decreed in 1938 that non-Germans of suitable 'Nordic' origin could enlist in the Allgemeine-SS, for at that point in time the distinction between the civilian 'general', or Allgemeine-SS, and 'military', or Waffen-SS, did not exist as such. Norway, Denmark, Holland and Belgium all had their own Fascist parties, which in some cases modelled themselves on Germany, for example, while other European countries took their

Left: Léon Degrelle, the leader of Walloon volunteers on the Eastern Front and winner of the Knight's Cross. Hitler told him: 'If I had a son, I would wish him to be like you.'

known as the 3rd Estonian SS Volunteer Brigade. Further volunteers were called up from Estonia, and in 1944 the 20th Waffen-Grenadier Division of the SS Estonian No 1 was formed. In the Western Ukraine, the local German authorities were deeply suspicious and only after overcoming considerable differences between themselves were volunteer units raised in 1943. This led to the formation of a new division 14th Waffen-Grenadier Division of the SS Galician No 1.

Missed opportunities

It should be added that the Cossack Corps was also assigned to the Waffen-SS. It had been organised in 1943 under General von Pannwitz, and during the summer of 1944 the two brigades were upgraded to become the 1st and 2nd Cossack Cavalry Division. In November 1944, the Waffen-SS announced its intention of taking over both and creating a larger formation to be known as XV Cossack Cavalry Corps. The German officers belonging to the corps, however, were not assigned to the Waffen-SS, only attached.

An enormous amount of goodwill and enthusiasm was wasted in these regions by the lack of planning and hesitation on the part of the German authorities. A greater number of volunteers could have been attracted in the Baltic States and the Ukraine if the German authorities had shown a positive and straightforward stance in 1941.

Strangely, given the racial policy of the SS, Muslim volunteers were recruited from the local population in Croatia and Albania. In early 1943, the first Croatian SS volunteer division was formed, which was reorganised into the 13th Waffen Mountain Division of the SS *Handschar* Croatian No 1. A second Croatian Division was formed, being designated 23rd Waffen Mountain Division of the SS *Kama* Croatian No 2, in the summer of 1944. The Albanian National Committee recruited for the Albanian forces, which were made up primarily from conscripts, with only a few volunteers. In the spring of 1944, in conjunction with other units, they raised a division which was later designated the 21st Waffen Mountain Division of the SS *Skanderbeg* Albanian No 1.

Other national units were formed, some of strategic merit, while others were of propaganda value only. These included two Russian divisions, the 29th Waffen-Grenadier Division of the SS Russian No 1 and the 30th Waffen-Grenadier Division of the SS Russian No 2, an Italian Waffen-Grenadier Division and a Hungarian, the 25th Waffen-Grenadier Division of the SS *Hunyadi* Hungarian No 1.

The British Freikorps

Finally, of more dubious value was the Tartar Waffen Mountain Brigade of the SS, an East Turkish Waffen-SS unit, the Serbian Volunteer Corps, two Romanian Waffen grenadier regiments, a Bulgarian Waffen-SS grenadier regiment, the Indian Legion, and the *Britische* Freikorps, which was the smallest unit of foreign volunteers.

The idea that prisoners of war could be persuaded to fight in an anti-Bolshevik legion was put forward by John Amery, the eldest son of Leo Amery, Churchill's Minister for India. The German Army was not receptive to the notion at first, as it was opposed to the recruitment of prisoners. A change of heart occurred, and Amery undertook a recruiting tour that yielded only one volunteer. The Germans decided to drop Amery, but not the idea of a British volunteer corps. The propaganda campaign was heightened, yielding about 58 volunteers who were assembled at Hildesheim. The name *Britische* Freikorps was adopted, with the intention that it would appear in October or November 1943. It was sent to Dresden to be trained as an assault engineer unit. In the course of the infamous 'fire storm' raid on the city, it suffered its first casualties when two of its members were killed. The *Britische* Freikorps was sent to Berlin in February 1945 and then assigned to the *Nordland* Division in March. On 13 April Cooper, the senior NCO in charge, went to the headquarters of the *Nordland* Division to discuss the *Britische* Freikorps with the commander, SS-Brigade-führer Ziegler. Cooper briefed Ziegler on the

Right: British Freikorps members, including a youthful Kenneth Berry (left) and Alfred Minchin (centre), complete with Union Jack arm shields and cuff bands. The unit was militarily insignificant.

background to the *Britische* Freikorps, emphasising that most of its members had been press-ganged into joining and that their combat value would be dubious. Ziegler agreed and Steiner's formal consent was sought to withdraw the *Britische* Freikorps from the frontline. Although withdrawn from a combat role the *Britische* Freikorps still had a job to do, and surprisingly enough it soldiered on, continuing with its work of driving trucks, directing traffic and helping with the evacuation of civilian refugees. On 29 April, Steiner told his staff of his decision to break contact with the Russians and ordered his forces to head west into Anglo-American captivity. The *Britische* Freikorps were duly captured and returned to Britain.

The balance sheet

The foreign volunteer programme remained central to the development of the Waffen-SS, but the value of their contribution to the war in Russia varied between excellent and very poor. In the case of the western European volunteers, the SS was able to tap a useful source of high-grade manpower, which the German armed forces would otherwise have found unavailable. The western volunteers fought well on the battlefield, the ultimate criterion for any military organisation. The SS had one major criticism levelled against it, as far as the western volunteers were concerned, which was the inability of its training grounds, officer and NCO schools to readily accommodate non-German recruits, a system weakness that was corrected far too slowly.

SS policy can only be seen as an almost unmitigated disaster with regard to the eastern European volunteers. Given the wide range of nationalities involved, the German suggestion that the invasion of the Soviet Union was a 'European' undertaking to rid the world of Communism was valuable propaganda. The

military evaluation is more critical. The small Finnish SS detachments were obviously good soldiers, but would have fought just as well in their own national institutions. The Baltic divisions also fought well, especially in the defence of their homelands, but the remaining units were poor.

The whole programme could have been excused in 1941 or perhaps even as late as 1942 for its propaganda potential, but in 1943, especially after the failure at Kursk, it siphoned off trained officers and NCOs desperately needed elsewhere at a time manpower and material shortages began to bite.

NEW TACTICS FOR A NEW WAR

With the failure of the Kursk Offensive, the Wehrmacht was forced onto the defensive in the East. The Red Army had successfully halted what was to be the last great German offensive on the Eastern Front, and was now poised to begin a massive attack all along the front. The Germans still hoped to maintain the 'Eastern Rampart', the deep defence lines that they hoped would hold the Russians indefinitely. It was upon this that the German High Command relied, a somewhat forlorn hope. The Russians, though, were confident and brimming with other ideas.

The Red Army's main effort was directed at the southern sector, where there were five fronts: Central, Voronezh, Steppe, Southwest and South. It had to push through the eastern Ukraine to reach and cross the River Dnieper. The Kalinin and West Fronts, situated father north, were tasked with pushing forward around Smolensk to hold down large German

Left: Waffen-SS infantry and armour in central Russia, August 1943. The vehicle is a StuG III Ausf G assault gun/tank destroyer armed with a 7.5cm gun.

forces which would be urgently needed elsewhere. STAVKA, the Soviet High Command, had learnt the art of balancing the actions of several fronts, and of establishing great local superiority in designated sectors. The tactical problems of breaking through deep and strongly fortified defensive lines had also been mastered the by Russians. A logistical system capable of re-supplying their armies during the advance to keep up the momentum had also been devised. This was particularly important, as the Germans had undertaken a 'scorched earth' policy, which laid waste towns and villages as they retreated.

After the Battle of Kursk, Red Army tactics focused on strategic and organisational flexibility, with heavy concentrations of artillery, and a broad frontage of attack. When the German line had been breached in one or two places, the main element of the attacking force was transferred into the gap for maximum exploitation. The Wehrmacht and Waffen-SS responded by trying to ensure that the initial Soviet assault struck empty space. They did this by withdrawing units immediately prior to the Red Army attack. To deal with Russian breakthroughs, they held back their tanks for counterattacks after anti-tank weapons had stopped the Russians in the main killing zones.

Tactics on the ground

Fortunately the Germans, and especially the Waffen-SS, had the soldiers for such tactics. On the northeastern front in February 1943, for example, SS-Untersturmführer Gerardus Mooyman, who had joining the SS Volunteer Legion *Nederland* as a gunner in the 14th Anti-tank Company, destroyed more than 15 Russian tanks south of Lake Ladoga with his anti-tank gun. In recognition of his gallantry, he became the first 'Germanic' volunteer in the Waffen-SS to be honoured with the award of the Knight's Cross of the Iron Cross, on 20 February 1943. General Major Fritz von Scholz decorated him personally on 17 March 1943. Subsequently, he was paraded for the press for propaganda purposes, first in Berlin, where he met Dutch journalists on 23 March. He made a number of other photo calls, and met SS-Gruppenführer Reuter and Seyss-Inquart in Holland to help with the recruiting programme in the Low Countries, as well as to bolster flagging morale at home.

Strongpoints were constructed by the German approximately 16km (10 miles) apart, which were expected to hold for 24 hours against Russian attacks. The German troops would then fall back to the next defence line (flank attacks could be launched against those Red Army units deployed to tackle each strongpoint). These tactics were sound, but the Russian advance could never be delayed more than temporarily with this strategy, albeit at heavy cost to Red Army units. The hope that the Red Army would, in Hitler's words, 'some day be exhausted' was totally unrealistic. The Red Army mustered 1400 tanks and over 20,000 artillery pieces during the battles to recapture Smolensk in August and September 1943, compared to the 500 tanks and 8800 artillery pieces the Germans could field.

Waffen-SS deployments

Throughout 1941-43, the élite divisions of the Waffen-SS, the *Leibstandarte* Division, *Das Reich* Division and *Totenkopf* Division, had displayed qualities which the Führer regarded as being essential to victory: a ruthless aggression in attack, with a stolid refusal ever to yield ground. It was perhaps inevitable, therefore, that he should look to these units to save the situation in the East after Kursk. The events in the Mediterranean at this time, however, gave Hitler cause for alarm. The Führer's worst fears concerning Italy were confirmed in the last week of July 1943, when Mussolini's regime finally crumbled. His old ally was placed under arrest, though, and Hitler immediately made plans for rescuing *Il Duce* and for strengthening the German hold on Italy. Marshal Badoglio's new government stated its intention of continuing the war, but no one at the Führer's headquarters, least of all Hitler, believed that. Hitler's initial plan was to transfer II SS Panzer Corps from Army Group South to Italy. He thought that the politically trained

Above: SS-Untersturmführer Geradus Mooyman (right) of the Dutch unit Legion Nederland with SS-Standartenführer Hank Feldmeyer. Mooyman won the Knight's Cross for knocking out 15 Russian tanks.

SS divisions could form a nucleus around which the Fascist elements in the Italian Army could rally. After consultation with the commander of Army Group Centre, Hitler decided to send only the II SS Panzer Corps headquarters and the *Leibstandarte* Division. The latter left its equipment, including its Mark IV and VI tanks, at the front to be divided among depleted divisions. Though the *Leibstandarte* Division was sent to Italy, *Das Reich* remained in the Army Group South zone. Subsequently *Das Reich*, the *Totenkopf* Division and III Panzer Corps were sent to Stalino to try to

stem the Russian offensive in that sector. But their respite was brief. Having achieved their objective at the beginning of August 1943, they were attacked by the Red Army on 3 August between Orel and Belgorod, which ripped a huge hole in the German line. To halt the collapse of Manstein's left flank, *Das Reich* and

Above: Waffen-SS troops on the retreat as Army Group Centre reels under relentless Russian pressure, autumn 1943. During this period the Das Reich *and* Totenkopf *Divisions fought superbly to prevent a German collapse.*

the *Totenkopf* Division were rushed to the Kharkov area. An attack at Belgorod fell like a thunder clap upon the forces of Hoth's 4th Panzer Army and Army Detachment *Kempf*. It was launched by the Soviet Voronezh and Steppe Fronts: five armies with a superiority in tanks and guns of five to one over the hapless Germans. The latter reeled backwards in total disarray, yielding Belgorod on 5 August. A 48km- (30-mile) wide gap soon appeared in the German line between Hoth's and Kempf's forces, into which the Red Army commander, General Vatutin, poured troops. Kharkov was bypassed by the Soviets, who then swung southwest towards Poltava. Their objective was to cut off Army Group South by taking the crossings over the River Dnieper between Kiev and Zaporozhye.

Field Marshal von Manstein ordered the two Waffen-SS divisions to repulse the Russian attack towards the River Dnieper and stop enemy armour from wheeling south and surrounding Army Detachment *Kempf*, which was holding Kharkov. West of the city, just south of Akhtyrka, the *Das Reich* and *Totenkopf* Divisions dug in and awaited the Red Army tanks. The Waffen-SS troops prevented the Russians reaching the River Dnieper, but endured ferocious assaults for seven days. Kempf's position became untenable in the city, and to escape encirclement he was forced to abandon Kharkov on 22 August. On Hitler's orders Manstein dismissed him from his command. Kempf's army was now placed under the command of General Otto Wöhler and redesignated the 8th Army. Wöhler's task was to rebuild the German front west of Kharkov, and he was greatly helped in this by the efforts of the *Das Reich* and *Totenkopf* Divisions. The *Totenkopf* spearheaded an action between 15 and 20 August to encircle and destroy Vatutin's lead elements, which were trying to encircle Kharkov from the west. The *Totenkopf* Division then linked up with the still intact 7th Panzer Division and thus re-established contact with the 4th Panzer Army. The two SS divisions then covered the retreat of the 8th Army, helping to avert a major German disaster.

Retreat to the Dnieper

The fact that the Germans would have to retreat to the natural defence line of the River Dnieper was recognised by Field Marshal Manstein and grudgingly accepted by Hitler in mid-September. The *Totenkopf* Division and *Das Reich* covered the retreat as the 4th Panzer and 8th Armies fell back to the river. However, the Russians had recommenced their attacks, and both Waffen-SS divisions were sorely pressed in preventing the Russians reaching the river as the German troops and vehicles poured over the crossing points. There was still to be no respite for the SS troops, who were now very tired. To the south, a crisis had developed where Russian forces had punched a hole in the German line between the right flank of Wöhler's 8th Army and the left wing of General Hube's 1st Panzer

Army. Krivoi Rog was the rail, supply and communications centre for Army Group South, and now it was in danger. Its loss would have dealt a mortal blow to Army Group South, as vast quantities of supplies were held there.

Below: A brief period of rest before the next frenzied efforts to stem the Red Army. This photograph provides a good example of the seemingly endless Russian terrain encountered on the Eastern Front.

Having smashed the 57th Army Corps and cut the rail link between Dnepropetrovsk and Krivoi Rog, by mid-October the Russians appeared to be within reach of the prize. A reserve force was desperately thrown together by Field Marshal von Manstein: Schörner's 40th Panzer Corps, which included the *Totenkopf* Division, the remnants of the 9th and 11th Panzer Divisions and the 16th Panzergrenadier Division. From north of Krivoi Rog, the 40th Panzer Corps counterattacked on 27 October 1943, spearheaded by the *Totenkopf* Division. After a week of bitter fighting, the Russians were stopped dead in their tracks, losing 500 tanks and 5000 prisoners. They then pulled back, allowing the evacuation of Krivoi Rog four months later, together with all the valuable supplies located there.

Left: Soldiers of the 4th SS-Polizei Division digging trenches on the Eastern Front. In March 1943, the nucleus of the division was transferred to Bohemia and Moravia for refitting as a panzer-grenadier division. This was part of a general pattern of upgrading many Waffen-SS divisions in an effort to try to contain the Red Army on the Eastern Front. Hitler, though faced with a grim strategic situation in Russia, was still convinced that the Waffen-SS could give him ultimate victory in Russia. This view was not shared by the troops at the front, and illustrates how detached Hitler had become from reality. The truth was that the Waffen-SS was stretched to the limit staving off defeat.

The expansion was in three areas. First, the élite Waffen-SS units, the *Leibstandarte*, *Das Reich* and *Totenkopf* Divisions, together with the *Wiking* Division, were to be upgraded to panzer divisions. Second, recognising that the war in the East could not be brought to a speedy end, it seemed sensible to increase the number of SS divisions of all types. Finally, Hitler decided that such was the worth of the best SS divisions that they should be formed into a central reserve, which would intervene in critical situations, such as at Kharkov in early 1943.

New Waffen-SS panzer divisions

The decision to increase the number of SS divisions was not taken lightly, for Hitler still wanted to preserve the exclusivity of the SS. However, Stalingrad forced him to authorise the creation of new divisions. On New Year's Eve 1942, Hitler agreed to the creation of two new armoured divisions, although originally they were designated as mechanised infantry divisions, numbered the 9th and 10th and named after two heroes of German military history. The division, which was later to be named 9th SS Panzer Division *Hohenstaufen*, was formed without name in January 1943. The second was simply identified as the 10th division of the Waffen-SS. In spite of the fact that Hitler did not like the name, the division was called 'Karl der Grosse' in April 1943. By 3 October 1943, Hitler named the unit after a historical figure more to his liking – 'Frundsberg' – and the division was now titled 10th SS Panzer Division *Frundsberg*. Himmler was forced to recruit native Germans for the first time to staff them. The third SS armoured division, the 12th SS Panzer Division *Hitlerjugend*, was created from the 1926 class of the Hitler Youth. In parallel to the additions to the Reichsdeutsch formations, a recruiting drive created the eastern European SS. Though undoubtedly necessary, it effectively destroyed Himmler's guidelines of racial selection.

The *Wiking* Division had remained on the defensive in the Caucasus during the winter of 1942-43 and into the following spring. On 22

The superior fighting qualities of the Waffen-SS divisions were proved time after time, but there was always a heavy price to pay. Hausser's II SS Panzer Corps lost over 400 tanks at Kursk alone. Such losses in equipment, in addition to that suffered in personnel, would have quickly exhausted the Waffen-SS had it not have been for Hitler's decision to substantially expand the organisation.

March, the *Nordland* Regiment was withdrawn from the division and used as a cadre for a new SS division. The Scandinavian regiment was merged with two existing SS Germanic legions and a large number of west and southeastern European volunteers to form the SS Freiwilligen-Panzergrenadier Division *Nordland*. During the summer the Estonian SS-Bataillon *Narwa* was attached to the *Wiking* Division where it remained until July 1944, when it was transferred to the Estonian 20th Waffen-Grenadier Division der SS. The summer and autumn found the division constantly on the defensive in the area from Kharkov to the River Dnieper.

Dedicated anti-Communist soldiers were needed to replace battle casualties, and units were needed to safeguard rear areas against partisans, who had sprung up everywhere in eastern Europe from 1942 onwards. This resulted in a plethora of different national groups wearing Waffen-SS uniform.

The Latvians raised the 15th Waffen-Grenadier Division der SS, which first fought on the Eastern Front in November 1943. It put up a spirited resistance against relentless Russian assaults, being driven westwards in the face of the Red Army. The Estonians, too, provided a rich seam of recruits for the SS.

The Waffen-SS comes of age

As the situation on the Eastern Front worsened, Hitler came to depend even more on his SS divisions. By the end of 1943, seven of his 30 panzer divisions were Waffen-SS and five of his panzergrenadier divisions wore SS uniforms. The *Leibstandarte* Division made the journey between East and West no less than seven times, making a major assault on each arrival. In November 1943, for example, newly returned from Italy, it led an assault which restored the Dnieper front.

By early February 1943, the retreating *SS-Polizei* Division took over its newly assigned position west of Kopino, where it had to repulse a number of fierce Russian onslaughts. With a lull along the whole front in March, the nucleus of the division was transferred to train-

ing areas in Silesia and Bohemia and Moravia for refitting as a panzergrenadier division. The remaining portions of the division had been reduced to the Battle Group *SS-Polizei*, which played a defensive role in the northern portion of the Eastern Front from April 1943 until 21 May 1944.

The massive expansion of the Waffen-SS from 1943 did not generally lead to a commensurate rise in military prowess. Those units which had been established before 1943 were without doubt the best, with the eastern European formations and Volksdeutsche varying in performance from very poor to excellent. The backbone of the Waffen-SS was its panzer divisions; their leadership, training, equipment and morale were such that they postponed the ultimate defeat of the Third Reich. The west European divisions – Danes, Dutch, Belgians, French and Norwegians – fought well, though numerically they formed the smallest group among Himmler's legions. Though theoretically a massive pool of recruits, the Volksdeutsche proved disappointing. Volksdeutsche personnel, it was said, used their alleged inability to understand the German language as an excuse to avoid unpleasant or dangerous assignments. Theodor Eicke was particularly scathing about them, even going as far as accusing them of cowardice. The barometer that could be used to gauge a Waffen-SS unit's military efficiency was usually the amount of Volksdeutsche personnel it contained: the greater the ratio the less its combat efficiency.

Despite all the efforts, the floodgates in the East burst open in 1944, and the Waffen-SS was caught in the deluge and swept west. Despite almost superhuman efforts, it could not carry out Hitler's wishes to hold the line; nor could it prevent the Russians reaching the very borders of the Third Reich itself.

Right: The strain begins to show. Fatigue was rife in the élite Waffen-SS divisions on the Eastern Front in the second half of 1943, as they were rushed from one trouble spot to another to deal with Red Army attacks.

CHAPTER 8

THE DIRTY WAR

As Hitler's élite troops, the Waffen-SS were charged with making the Führer's dream of racial purity come true. In the East, there were two main strands to this dream: the extermination of the Jews and the destruction of Bolshevism. The Einsatzgruppen were established prior to the invasion of Poland. The Führer's social plan for Poland was simple, radical and horribly effective: the liquidation of the country's cultural and political élite; it was also to be the testing ground for the larger plan – the destruction of the Jews and other 'undesirables' who inhabited the Soviet Union. With the conquest of Russia, Hitler's dream of racial purity for the world and the eradication of Bolshevism, 'a social criminality' in his mind, could be achieved.

The SS was also charged with the conduct of the anti-partisan war in the East and the Balkans. Initially, the responsibility for combating the partisan menace had rested with the army, but control was given to the Waffen-SS in October 1942, with SS-Obergruppenführer und General der Waffen-SS und Polizei Erich von dem Bach-Zelewski designated Chief of Anti-Partisan Warfare. He was given the title of Bevollmächtiger für die Bandenbekämpfung im Osten, or Plenipotentiary for the Combating of Partisans in the East. In 1943 this was changed to Chef der Bandenkampfverbände, or Chief of Anti-Partisan Formations.

Left: Suspected partisans and collaborators hanged by the Germans in Volokolamsk, near Moscow, in the winter of 1941. Bodies were left hanging as a warning to others.

Bach-Zelewski was senior SS and police leader in the Central Army Group area in Russia during 1941-2, and it was during this time he was involved in the liquidation of Jews and Bolsheviks. On becoming head of all anti-partisan units, he was directly responsible to Himmler himself.

Throughout the period of their spectacular triumphs in the Soviet Union, the German forces were also fighting a second campaign: a savage phantom war against the partisans. It was not a conflict which began spontaneously, for large sections of the population greeted the Germans who drove deep into the Soviet Union in 1941 as liberators who would free them from the Stalinist yoke.

The partisans – a shaky start

Before the war, while still in the process of communising the country, the Soviet Government had been totally opposed to the concept of 'a nation in arms'. Thus at first any resistance movements that were in place did not take up arms against the invaders, but acted simply as couriers and agents. Their numbers were small and they possessed sophisticated techniques, which required considerably ingenuity on the part of the security police to track them down.

Many Russian people adopted a 'wait and see attitude' about whether their government would survive or not. In fact, in the beginning there were two collaborators for every partisan. But the growth of the partisan movement was helped by the ruthlessness of the Russian guerrilla organisation towards collaborators, and by the savagery meted out by the Germans in the occupied areas.

There was no special equipment available or stocks of weapons, clothing, food and medical supplies. Neither the many experienced partisans who had participated in the Russian Civil War of 1918-21, nor those who had fought in the Spanish Civil War, were employed against the Germans. Indeed, many had been discredited as 'enemies of the people' and shot in the purges. The absence of training for partisan warfare, both theoretical and practical, togeth-er with the lack of any clear thought as to how the leadership should be organised, led to disagreement between the Soviet leaders early in the war. Some insisted on the creation of large formations, which should operate in accordance with the plans of the central military leadership. Others held the view that numerous small detachments receiving only general coordination and support from the High Command would prove more effective.

On 29 June 1941, the Central Committee of the Communist Party and the Soviet Government in Moscow issued a belated call to arms, in a directive that first gave reference to the need to organise partisan and sabotage activity in German-occupied territory. It was addressed to all party and government bodies in the western districts of the country, and in a radio speech delivered by Stalin on 3 July the entire population was called upon: 'To set up partisan cavalry and infantry detachments and sabotage groups in enemy occupied areas for the struggle against units of the enemy army, to inflame partisan warfare everywhere and at all times, to blow up bridges and roads, to spoil telephone communications, to set fire to forests, warehouses and wagons, to create unbearable conditions in the occupied areas for the enemy and all who helped him, to pursue and destroy them at every step, to disrupt everything they do.'

The defence of Mother Russia

At the same time, the directive demanded the establishment of 'destroyer' battalions, formed from the most loyal members of the civilian population and charged with preventing panic and disorganisation in areas near the front: 'We must organise a merciless struggle against all disorganisers of our rear, deserters, alarmists, rumour-mongers, and destroy spies, saboteurs, and enemy paratroops, cooperating speedily with our destroyer battalions in all this. The war with Nazi Germany must not be looked on as an ordinary war. It is not merely a war between two armies, it is also a great war of the whole Soviet people against the German forces.'

This was not only a call to the people to develop partisan warfare in the rear of the German forces, but also a threat that those who did not participate in the 'war of the whole Soviet people' would be regarded as traitors.

However, Stalin's speech did not arouse or inspire the Soviet people. No spontaneous anti-German movement arose in the occupied areas, so organisation of a partisan movement only continued along two lines: through the party organisation and that of the secret police. The Germans, on the other hand, made somewhat better use of local groups opposed either to Stalin's government or to the racially dominated 'Muscovite' Russians, who provided the troops for anti-partisan operations. The terrain in the Soviet Union was rarely as favourable for partisan operations as it was in Yugoslavia, but the sheer cruelty of the German occupation eventually fanned a vigorous resistance movement into life and alienated many who were potential allies.

German organisation in the East

Yet despite the killings, the deportations and imposition of a brutal military occupation, the Germans had little difficulty in finding volunteers to act as auxiliaries and behind-the-line security troops. The most enthusiastic of these were the non-Slavic people on the periphery of the Soviet Union: the Balts, Caucasians, Georgians, Turkomens and Cossacks. As the war progressed, they were joined by Ukrainians and Russians, and in many Ukrainian and Russian towns the action groups found willing helpers among the racial Germans, indigenous self-defence forces and militia. After the first wave of action, the Special Action Groups settled down to maintain security in the newly occupied territories, where they set up a static territorial organisation, which was in fact a miniature Reich Central Security Department (RSHA) in the field, with SD, Gestapo and Kripo (Criminal Police) representatives under a Commander of Security Police and SD. Under each commander were a number of local commanders of Security Police and SD. Towards the end of the

Above: Erich von dem Bach-Zelewski, senior SS and Police Leader in Army Group Centre's area in Russia. Head of all anti-partisan units, he had a nervous breakdown in 1942 due to the atrocities committed in Russia.

war, it was estimated that as many as a million citizens from the Soviet Union had taken up arms against their Communist government

On 18 July 1941, the Communist Party Central Committee issued a directive on organising the struggle in the rear of the German

forces. It ordered that underground party committees be set up on occupied territory, with the job of ensuring that partisan and subversive activity was developed in their areas. Responsibility for this was laid on local party and government leaders, especially on first secretaries of party organisations. The directive ordered the immediate preparation of underground party bodies and partisan detachments in areas close to the front, and the selec-

tion of the most loyal persons in the area to staff them.

Partisan detachments of 75-100 men, and sabotage groups of 30-50 men were to be organised primarily in areas where main enemy forces were concentrated, but it was intended to have at least one of each in every administrative division. The main targets for partisan detachments were columns and garrisons of enemy motorised infantry, transport

Left: Immediately following the Wehrmacht into Russia in June 1941 came the Einsatzgruppen, the SS Special Action Groups, intent on liquidating Communists, Jews, 'undesirables' and anyone else who fell foul of SS racial guidelines. Each Einsatzgruppe numbered less than 3000 men and a few women, and one wonders how they managed to murder nearly 500,000 Jews and gypsies alone during the first six months of the Russian Campaign, in addition to numerous Russian commissars who were captured. However, they were enthusiastically helped in their grisly task by locally raised volunteer units, especially in Latvia, Lithuania and Estonia.

Soviet forces also interacted with the German forces, adding to the final destruction of Poland. The Soviets had a plan for the destruction of the Polish officer corps and other intellectuals, and this led to vast numbers of deportations and executions. On 13 April 1943, Radio Berlin announced that a mass grave of 10,000 Polish officers had been discovered in Katyn Forest near Smolensk. They had been methodically and expertly shot by pistol in the back of the head by the NKVD (Russian Secret Police) in the spring of 1940. The German report was somewhat inaccurate – in fact 4500 Polish officers whom the Russians had failed to indoctrinate were murdered.

Retribution

The urban counterparts of the partisan detachments and sabotage groups were the networks of conspiratorial groups and agents established by the Communist Party, plus independent networks set up by the Internal Affairs and State Security Services. Their tasks were sabotage, terrorism and intelligence, and they often posed as collaborators in order to penetrate German military and administrative installations, preserving strict secrecy and avoiding contact with the partisans. One example is recorded in *The Moscow Tram Stop* and gives an account of a prominent young female partisan who was active in late 1941. She was interrogated by the German army and subsequently given duties at headquarters. An attractive girl, she soon won the favours of her new friends. But 'Tanya' was exposed and taken out by the Germans with a plaque round her neck proclaiming her crimes, hanged publicly in front of an audience of soldiers and left as a stark reminder to others. Group hangings were not uncommon. A small boy was shot through the head for possessing a pigeon and his body put on display. In the early months of the war, about 70 per cent of partisans were party or youth league members; because of their inexperience many of them, especially the active Communists, were captured and killed.

Desertion was a serious problem for the Soviets everywhere. In Smolensk Province, for

in general, airfields, and communications. For the sabotage groups, the main targets were telephone lines, stores of war material, small groups of soldiers, single lorries and tanks, the killing of officers, seizure of documents, and the spreading of rumours aimed at causing uncertainty and alarm among enemy troops. The killing of officers was a very high priority, for it was a prime objective of Stalinist ideals. During the Polish Campaign, for example, the example, over 6000 party and youth league members remained to operate in the German rear. But only 2000 were operational in 40 partisan detachments in the area by the autumn of 1941. And although 75 destroyer battalions, with a strength of 10,000, were raised in Orel province before the arrival of the Germans, only 2300 remained when they arrived, and during the ensuing three weeks some detachments disintegrated altogether, while others moved into Soviet-controlled territory.

Many soldiers who hid in towns, villages and forests in large numbers became apathetic after separation from their units. A partisan commander later wrote: 'Our Communists lost heart and some took conspiratorial activity to determine how best to hide themselves.' Anti-German activity was limited in these circumstances. Even the mighty Bryansk Forest only housed some 2500 partisans in the the first few months of the war.

The partisans of the Moscow region provided something of an exception. A staff of the partisan movement, 12 underground district committees and 40 partisan detachments with their bases were set up before the German forces reached the area. They had a hard core of 1500 party members, plus 300 members of the Youth League. They operated actively, attacking even German garrisons, and suffered heavy casualties as a result.

Increased partisan activity

The Germans had under their control about 70,000,000 Russian people by December 1941. At this time there were only about 30,000 partisans in this region, but this rapidly rose to an approximate 80,133 men organised in 661 detachments by 1 July 1942. The level of activity was still deemed unsatisfactory by the Soviet Central Staff, and on 1 August 1942 an immediate increase was demanded to aid the troops at the front. An amnesty was proclaimed on 12 August for all collaborators who ended their activities, while partisan commanders were ordered to kill those who continued.

The Belorussian and Bryansk Forest partisans responded by blowing up strongly guard-

ed railway bridges over the rivers Desna, Ptich and Drissa, together with other railway installations. The German General Directorate of Railway 'East' reported that due to partisan action, accidents increased from 90 in March to 180 in June, 315 in August and 342 in September, and from August 1942 approximately 200 locomotives were neutralised every month. The increased activity reduced train speeds, movements by night, and led to an increase in patrols and the building of fortifications on important bridges and main lines.

The Kovpak and Saburov Brigades

The scale of partisan activity was the focus of high-level discussion in Moscow at the end of August 1942, when about 20 commanders of the largest partisan brigades were summoned to a conference on subversive activity by the Central Staff. Stalin received the group on 31 August, which also conferred in the Kremlin with the Soviet leaders, who stated: 'The partisan movement, despite its obvious successes, has not yet become as massive as it could be.' They were ordered to create new partisan reserves in every village, and to direct efforts primarily against the Germans' long lines of communication.

The two largest brigades, commanded by S. Kovpak and A. Saburov, with over 1000 men, raided from the Bryansk Forests to the west bank of the Dnieper and on to the thinly wooded southwestern Ukraine. The main German communication lines lay in these regions. The raids had three distinct objectives: to create a diversion, to represent Soviet power, and to inflame the population against the Germans. At the end of October, the Kovpak and Saburov Brigades moved out, after being supplied by air with food, clothing, weapons, explosives, radios and portable printing presses. The important Ukrainian railway junction of Sarny was attacked, plus five bridges leading near it, were blown up by Kovpak's Brigade in December. Kovpak's Brigade was encircled by the Germans during a raid into the western Ukraine in summer 1943. Vershigora, head of intelligence, suggested that it should break out

in small groups, taking different directions and assemble in an appointed place later, but many partisan leaders did not trust their men enough to permit them to disperse. The brigade commissar rejected the plan, though, because it would destroy the team, which had been created and held together by strict discipline over two years.

A number of small, passive partisan detachments existed, which contributed little to the struggle. These were compelled to integrate with active units for the sake of discipline and energetic action. In some cases their commanders refused, preferring an easy existence in the village or forest hide-outs. These commanders were shot and their units forcibly integrated. Penetration by German agents and collaborators was minimised by the institution of

Above: Suspected partisans being led away following a German anti-guerrilla sweep in the Bryansk area in 1943. Guilty or not, all of them would be shot by firing squad after a series of brutal interrogations.

rigorous checks on new recruits. The latter carried out only auxiliary duties performed under constant surveillance. If it transpired they had an 'unclean' past or had behaved disloyally, they and their families were shot, their property confiscated or destroyed, and their houses burned.

Army Group Centre's communications were the priority of the Bryansk Forest partisans, who even undertook a joint operation in February 1943 with the Bryansk Front air forces. The air force attacked the stations,

large numbers of Poland's population. Eicke gave Berger the title of Höhere SS und Polizei Führer HSSPF, or Higher SS and Police Leader, for the regions of Poland, making him accountable to Himmler alone for his measures in 'pacifying' the conquered areas.

A trusted Eicke subordinate, SS-Standartenführer Paul Nostitz, commander of the SS-Totenkopf Standarte *Brandenburg*, carried out his orders thoroughly and fanatically. On 13 September *Brandenburg* moved into Poland to begin 'cleansing and security measures', which provided a fitting introduction to the character of German rule during the three weeks it was on active duty in Poland (and was an ominous foretaste of things to come in the Baltic States and Soviet Union). They secured villages from 'insurgents', conducted house searches and arrested large numbers of 'suspicious elements'. SS-Standartenführer Nostitz eagerly described in his report how insurgents, plunderers, Poles and Jews were quickly liquidated in large numbers, many of whom were shot 'while trying to escape'.

The disgust of the army

The 'cleansing and security measures' that occurred during and after the Polish Campaign engendered an attitude of uneasiness, shock and disgust among responsible senior officers of the German Army. General Boehm-Tettelbach recorded these feelings in his report to the 8th Army, in which he remarked that *Brandenburg* had the prime objective of taking violent action against the Jews. Nostitz's repeated refusal to perform normal security duties was cited to support his claims. The general also highlighted how SS-Gruppenführer Pancke had said openly that the SS had special tasks to perform that were outside the competence of the army, and therefore the SS-Totenkopfverbände would not obey army orders. The reports undoubtedly reached Colonel-General Blaskowitz, who loathed the Death's Head units. His knowledge of the atrocities committed transformed him into the army's most bitter critic of SS behaviour in Poland. As a protest, he composed a long mem-

orandum cataloguing the crimes committed by the SS-Totenkopfverbände in Poland and sent it to Generaloberst von Brauchitsch, the German Army Commander-in-Chief.

German soldiers began to question the activities of the SS. Because of this, the SS's heinous enterprises were often camouflaged by such euphemisms as 'counter-espionage work' in an attempt to keep them secret from their own regular forces.

Preparations for Russia

The 14th Army's operational section reported on 20 September 1939 that the 'troops are especially incensed that instead of fighting at the front young men should be demonstrating their courage against defenceless civilians'. In the Operational Zone the Einsatzgruppen were technically under army command, and more than one senior Wehrmacht officer became worried by the consequences. Admiral Wilhelm Canaris, the Chief of the Abwehr, or military intelligence, told the High Command: 'the world will one day hold the Wehrmacht responsible for these methods, since these things are taking place under its nose.' But most generals were prepared to turn a blind eye to the dirty work of the SS.

At the end of March 1940, the German military machine was swept into a new and terrible 'planning phase' when Hitler revealed what his 'crusade against Bolshevism' involved. On 30 March, in a two-and-a-half-hour speech, Hitler addressed the commanders of the three services and some 250 senior officers selected for 'Barbarossa', and made plain his commitment to a war of extermination, not merely a conquest. In this gigantic clash of ideology, knightly virtues would have no place, for Bolshevism was 'a social criminality'. All Bolshevik commissars and Communist intelligentsia must be put to death, and no personal scruple could stand in the way.

Himmler had been granted substantial and independent powers over occupied territory in the East, and on 3 March took responsibility for 'certain tasks which stem from the necessity finally to settle the conflict between the two

On the blackboard: *Gustav der Eiserne spricht: „Je mehr Dienst desto grösser die Ehre ist."*

Above: Members of an auxiliary unit raised to assist the Einsatzgruppen with uniformed German police officer in the Ukraine. Note the skull in front of the blackboard, no doubt provided by one of the unit's victims.

opposing political systems'. The 'Instructions on Special Matters', (Annexe to Directive 21), the OKW directive of 13 March 1941, laid down Himmler's special freedom of action, and decreed the division of occupied Russia into 'ethnographic areas' following the army group divisions: Baltic, Belorussia and Ukraine. Each was to be ruled by Reichskommissars, who were to take over as rapidly as possible. Their responsibility lay directly to the Führer, and the coordination of 'the economic administration' of military operational and rear administrative zones alike was assigned to Göring. Military rule exercised by the army was therefore severely limited in both time and scope

The 'special tasks' would be carried out in the military rear and General Wagner, Quartermaster General, discussed with Heydrich the terms of the relationship between the military and SD. On 26 March 1940, a draft order covering this arrangement and the eventual operations of the Einsatzgruppen in the army's rear areas was published. Hitler's speech put Communist Party commissars, officials, military personnel and civilians beyond any law, save one which automatically sentenced them to summary execution. Commissars when captured would be shot out

Left: 'Here he stops at nothing, and in his vileness he becomes so gigantic that no one need be surprised if among our people the personification of the devil as the symbol of all evil assumes the living shape of the Jew.' (Hitler: Mein Kampf) In Nazi eyes the Slavs and Jews battled for top spot in the list of 'sub-humanity'. The result was murder on a mass scale once the war in the East began. Himmler was informed on 23 March 1943 that 633,000 Jews, such as the one shown here, in Russia had been 'resettled', the euphemism for extermination. With regard to the Slav, the SS issued a brochure entitled The Sub-Human which stated: '[the sub-human] is a frightful creature, a caricature of a man with features similar to those of a human being but intellectually and morally lower than any animal.' This Jewish man has been dressed in religious robes prior to being shot.

of hand, if not by German combat troops then by the Einsatzgruppe to whom they would be handed over, or, as the draft of the infamous Commissar Order put it: 'Political leaders and commissars who are captured will not be sent to the rear.'

Another directive on the 'coordinated execution' of 'special tasks' in the East was published at the end of March. The army's first Special Directives, dated 3 April, was issued by General Wagner on this basis, restricting the army's responsibility to its already limited zone. The boundaries of the military conscience had also to be fixed or forgotten. Further wrangling between the SS and OKW took place before an agreement which stated that 'the Einsatzgruppen are authorised, within the framework of their task and on their own responsibility, to take executive measures affecting the civilian population'. The zones and conditions in which the Einsatzgruppen could operate were laid down by General-oberst von Brauchitsch, the Commander-in-Chief of the Army, on 28 April 1941. The operational zones were divided into four, with an Einsatzgruppe in each: Einsatzgruppe A, assigned to operations in Latvia, Lithuania and Estonia and commanded by SS-Gruppenführer Stahlecker; B, assigned to the Baltic states and the Ukraine, commanded by SS-Gruppenführer Nebe; C, assigned to the Ukraine south of B, commanded by SS-Oberführer Rasch; and D, taking the remainder of the Ukraine, commanded by SS-Gruppenführer Ohlendorf. The order also empowered them to take executive measures against civilians as long as they did not interfere with military operations.

The first atrocities

A number of different departments, offices and units of the SD, Waffen-SS and Order Police provided personnel for the Einsatzgruppen, which were armed with light automatic weapons. Vast distances were covered by the fully motorised Einsatzgruppen, which followed so closely in the wake of the advancing German troops that often SD and Gestapo personnel became involved in the fighting.

In the days following the invasion, one of the first atrocities occurred on the Soviet frontier at the village of Virbalis. Along a 5km (3.12-mile) length of anti-tank trench, Jews were forced to lie down before being exterminated by machine-gun fire. This was repeated seven times. The children were spared, only to be held by the legs, their heads smashed against stones, and then buried alive.

Mass murder

The Einsatzgruppen fanned out behind the frontline, which had by now penetrated deep into the Soviet Union. Here they killed with a ferocity and intensity all who came into their clutches: political functionaries or commissars, active Communists, looters, saboteurs, agents of the NKVD, traitorous ethnic Germans, 'unwanted' elements, carriers of epidemics, members of Russian partisan bands, armed insurgents, partisan helpers, rebels, agitators, young vagabonds, and Jews in general. The licence given to the Einsatzgruppen for their programme of slaughter appeared to know no bounds.

A look at the Einsatzgruppen commanders gives a depth to the enormity of the horrors wreaked upon the occupied territories. SS-Gruppenführer Franz-Walter Stahlecker, for example, was an 'information officer' in the SD in 1938 and went on to become Head of Section VIa of the Reich Main Security Office. At the beginning of 1942 Heydrich got rid of Stahlecker by dubiously promoting him to the command of Einsatzgruppe A. Heydrich's reports claimed that Stahlecker's group had liquidated 221,000 victims. It is possible, however, that such figures were reached carelessly, with the same totals being added several times over. Heydrich nevertheless would have benefited from this misrepresentation, firstly by demonstrating his personal success in the 'Final Solution', and secondly to neutralise Nebe, who is said to have fought against Heydrich's orders. These calculations allowed Himmler to contrast Nebe's quite 'modest' score of 46,000 executions against Stahlecker's massive 221,000.

Transcripts of German police radio messages, the so-called 'Incident Reports' detailing the massacre of thousands of Soviet Jews, show that the German Ordnungspolizei (Orpo) – the uniformed Order Police – were massacring Jews as early as June 1941, several months before the 'Final Solution' was thought to have begun.

During the summer of 1941, the Einsatzgruppen commanders radioed a triumphal tally of their killings back to Berlin. The most horrifying figures were in the last week of August, when 12,361 Ukrainian Jews were executed. Another report, from Lithuania, stated that 'about 500 Jews, among other saboteurs, are currently being liquidated every day'. Most were killed by police rather than the SS. The Ordnungspolizei messages dried up in September after Daluege, Chief of Police, warned his commanders that the enemy might be listening and told them to send details of all future 'executions' to Berlin by courier. On 19 December 1941, a report from Einsatzgruppe B stated: 'In checks on the exit roads from Ogilev, carried out with the assistance of the Ordnungspolizei, a total of 135 people, most of them Jews, were seized.'

Murderous ingenuity

In May 1942, the Commander of Security Police and SD in Lublin formed a Sondereinsatzgruppe, or 'Special Action Group', which was to disguise itself as a partisan band and assist the security forces in the maintenance of order. This unit was intended to carry out large-scale looting and reprisals in the name of the partisans, and thus discredit the partisan movement in the eyes of the local inhabitants. It also took part in anti-Jewish operations. On 23 July 1942, the police chief in Kamenetz reported that in 'the Jewish action, 700 incapable of working have been shot'.

But large-scale death by shooting had had its day. By the winter of 1941-42 the Einsatzgruppen leaders were feeling the effects of the murders. Nebe was a mere shadow of himself and on the verge of a nervous breakdown. Himmler travelled to Minsk to encourage his executioners, but when he attended a shooting he nearly collapsed. SS-Obergruppenführer Bach-Zelewski pressed Himmler to reserve any momentary sympathy not for the victims, but for the executioners who had to carry out such work. Shortly after this visit Himmler instructed Nebe to develop another method of killing. Nebe agreed, for the psychological effect on those who had to carry out the executions was very great. He began experimenting with killing people, in one case 80 inhabitants of a lunatic asylum, using exhaust gas from his car, an eight-cylinder Horch. He went about the task with an enthusiasm that he was incapable of keeping to himself. He was a keen amateur film maker, and after the war footage showing a gas chamber, worked by the exhaust of a lorry, was found in his Berlin flat.

Auxiliary units

Not only was the destruction of life the primary objective of the SS, but the confiscation of property and valuables belonging to its victims in the conquered states was also of paramount importance. SS-Obergruppenführer Joachim von Ribbentrop, the German Foreign Minister, commanded a special SS battalion which plundered works of art and sent them back to Berlin. The messages also give a clue to the disappearance of the legendary Amber Room, looted from one of the Tsar's palaces near Leningrad by the Germans. They refer to a 'Special SS Battalion' set up to loot treasures from occupied countries, being responsible for dismantling the gold and amber-clad room and taking it to Germany, where it later disappeared before the Allies invaded.

The auxiliary police units were first established by the German Army. The Einsatzgruppen following closely behind immediately took over the existing auxiliary units, or formed their own with recruits from ethnic

Right: The executioners toy with one of their victims during the SS's war against 'sub-humanity' in Russia. This Jew will make his way to a large pit to be shot; he will be but one of hundreds, maybe thousands.

Germans, pro-Germans in general, and reliable members of the defunct Soviet militia. They had various names, such as Ortsmiliz, Miliz, Ordnungsdienst, Bürgerwehr and Selbstschutz. Once the Einsatzgruppen became static, auxil-iaries were deployed primarily as interpreters and guards, while the Order Police absorbed some of the rank and file. The indigenous pop-ulation continued to be the subject of recruit-ment by both police and army, who employed

Above: Eager civilians in Latvia or Estonia receive orders from an auxiliary about the digging of graves to hold the corpses of Jews. It is a sad fact that Nazism tapped a rich anti-Semitic vein in the Soviet Union.

them in similar roles and later as anti partisan fighters. These units were often unreliable, being haphazardly formed, ill-disciplined, badly equipped and poorly trained.

The situation behind the front deteriorated to such an extent, particularly in Belorussia's heavily wooded regions, that guidelines for combating the partisan menace in the eastern territories had to be issued by OKW. It was the first official recognition that Soviet citizens had been trained and armed to fight in the rear of the German forces.

According to Himmler's orders of 6 November 1941, all auxiliaries were to be mustered into auxiliary police units. These were known as Schutzmannschaften, officially abbreviated to Schutz.-Btl., or more commonly Schuma. Btl. These battalions were placed at the disposal of the Order Police commander and the HSSPF (Higher SS Police Force). A six-month engagement was stipulated for recruits from Estonia, Latvia, Lithuania and Ukraine.

The Reichskommissars

The Ministry for Occupied Eastern Territories received the administration of the areas behind the front from the military, and began to incorporate four massive Reichskommissariat. However, the military situation at the front dictated that only two were actually created: Reichskommissariat Ostland, consisting of Estonia, Latvia, Lithuania, Belorussia, and much of the Ukraine; and the Reichskommissariat Ukraine itself.

Heinrich Lohse was appointed Reichskommissar of Reichskommissariat Ostland, and HSSPF Ostland was SS-Obergruppenführer und General der Polizei Friedrich Jeckeln. With the occupation of Estonia, Army Group North established a Selbstschutz, or 'self-defence' region. With normalisation of conditions, the Selbstschutz was reorganised on territorial lines. Reval, Harrien, Jerwen, Wierland, Narwa, Dorpat, Werro, Walk, Petschur, Pernau Fellin, Ösel and Wiek were established as self-defence regions in July 1942. Selbstschutzgebietsführer, or 'Regional Self-Defence Leaders', were also appointed to

command each region, and were subordinate to the Police Prefect. All Estonia's railway territory was formed into a railway region in July 1944 and was subordinate to the Railway Prefect. With the exception of those employed in the war economy, Estonians who were physically fit and between the ages of 17 and 45 were eligible for compulsory service. An Estonian Security Police comprising five departments also existed in Reval. Estnische Sicherungsabteilungen, or 'Estonian Security Battalions', were formed at the end of 1941, being re-titled 'Schuma battalions' in 1942

Above: The work of the Einsatzgruppen went on regardless of the weather. However, by the end of 1942 shooting as a method of mass extermination in the East was giving way to the gassing of victims.

A former police captain named Petersen commanded the Latvian Auxiliary Police force, which had been raised on 3 July 1941 and numbered 240 men in six police districts by 16 July 1941. These had been either former police constables, soldiers or members of the Aizsargi, a 'self-defence' organisation founded during the Ulmanis dictatorship in 1934. Eventually, the various auxiliary units were all amalgamated to form the Lettische Sicherungs-abteilungen, or 'Latvian Security Battalions', in November 1941, which were renamed Schuma Battalions in 1942

The German Field Commandant's office ordered that all anti-Soviet partisans in and around Kovno in Lithuania be disbanded on 28 June 1941. Five auxiliary companies were then formed from more reliable elements. The Jewish concentration camp at Kovno was guarded by one company, while another under-took police duties. In Wilna the Lithuanian political police was disbanded in July 1941, with the Ordnungsdienst (Order Service), con-sisting of about 150 men, being affiliated to the Einsatzgruppen. The Lithuania Security Battalion was formed at the end of 1941, prob-ably from Order Service personnel and auxil-iary police.

In 1939, a new Belorussian police force replaced the old organisation after it had been thoroughly purged. However, as the German Army approached it fled, destroying its records. The Germans formed auxiliary police from Polish and Belorussian criminal police officials, which were used by the German Security Police in Bialystok. It is also thought that a number of Belorussian auxiliary security police units existed. In Belorussia itself, the first Ukrainian Schuma Battalion was formed on 24 August 1941.

Reichskommissariat Ukraine

The second region, Reichskommissariat Ukraine, was under Reichskommissar Erich Koch, with HSSPF Russland-Süd under SS-Obergruppenführer und General der Waffen-SS und Polizei Erich von dem Bach-Zelewski. A Ukrainian Security Service was found to exist in Cherson by the Germans. Unreliable ele-ments were weeded out and subsequently 157 men were ceremoniously sworn in. Tasked with guarding factories and stores against loot-ers, saboteurs and what was euphemistically called 'the maintenance of peace', it was also responsible for rounding up Jews. Ethnic

Germans were obliged to report to the unit and about 180 had complied by 10 September 1942. Identity papers were issued and they were then employed as specialists and inter-preters. To maintain order, a Ukrainian self-defence militia was also established, with the first Schuma Battalions being raised in August 1941; they reached a strength of 14,452 men by February 1942. The Ukrainian police unit *Murrawa* was attached to the 30th Waffen-Grenadier Division (Russian No 2) in July 1944 as the 23rd Security Service Battalion for a short time.

One of the reasons the Germans were able to raise sizeable units relatively quickly after their invasion of the Soviet Union was the wide-scale dissatisfaction, even hatred, felt towards the Moscow régime.

Kaminiski's kingdom

Waffen-Brigadeführer Bronislav Vladislavovich Kaminiski, for example, was born in St Petersburg, the son of a Polish father and German mother. A chemical engineer by pro-fession, Kaminiski had no reason to love the Soviets. Under suspicion as a 'foreigner', bour-geois intellectual and potential dissident, he had spent five years in one of Stalin's labour camps, having been released only a few months before the German invasion. He was a brilliant, if autocratic, organiser who spoke German fluently and threw himself whole-heartedly behind the German cause. He tried, unsuccessfully, to form a Russian Nazi party, but apart from this one failure his record was one of unqualified success.

In January 1942 the town of Lokot fell under the jurisdiction of the 2nd Panzer Army. It stood on the edge of the Bryansk Forest, about halfway between Orec and Kursk in central Russia. It became a model of self-sufficiency under his guidance, having its own newspa-pers, hospitals, banks and even its own Kaminiski-devised tax system. The stipulated food supplies never failed to be delivered to the Wehrmacht on time, and the Germans found it necessary to maintain only a minimum liaison staff. The original self-defence force of

500 men was expanded into a small private army, which by September 1943 had grown into a brigade of some 10,000 men organised in five infantry regiments, supported by its own artillery of 36 field guns and armour comprising 24 captured Soviet T-34 tanks, as well as engineer, signals and medical units. This force went under the grandiose title of the 'Russian Liberation People's Army', or RONA.

The RONA fought several successful actions against the partisans of Bryansk, and even induced some of them to change sides. Kaminiski was dubbed 'the War Lord of the Bryansk Forest'. By the autumn of 1943 the Germans were in continuous retreat in Russia, and it was not long before Lokot had to be evacuated in the face of the Red Army's relentless advance. Kaminiski and his RONA, which now comprised some 15,000 men, were removed to Ratibor on the Polish-Czech border, taking with it a train of 10,500 civilians and 1500 cows.

In March 1944 the RONA was renamed a Volksheer Brigade, or 'People's Brigade'. In July it was accepted into the Waffen-SS proper as SS Assault Brigade RONA. Kaminiski was granted a commission as a Waffen-Brigade-führer. His men were not, as yet, deemed fit for frontline service, and were sent for further training to Hungary.

Deflated 'Zeppelin'

Operation 'Zeppelin', an attempt to raise large units for special operations behind the Soviet lines, was conceived in 1942. Under the command of SS-Obersturmbannführer Dr Gräfe, selected SS leaders were attached to RSHA Amt VI C, who toured prisoner-of-war camps in occupied Russian territory from March until June 194 to encourage Red Army soldiers to work against the Soviets, with promises of a modicum of freedom and better conditions. A unit of former inmates was established in April 1942 with the initial purpose of broadcasting subversive propaganda to their erstwhile comrades. By the end of the year, this project had been re-evaluated to encompass parachuting suitably trained Russian agents into Russia to act as saboteurs in the enemy rear. This led to the establishment of three units – North, Central and South – which were tasked with information-gathering and the organisation of subversion and sabotage. Sizeable numbers of recruits came forward, but due to lack of sufficient aircraft no really large-scale operations were ever undertaken. Thus the original purpose of 'Zeppelin', the deployment of large units in the Soviet rear, had been thwarted, which prompted the decision to employ the majority of the personnel recruited in anti-partisan operations.

SS Verband Druzhina

A combat unit was formed and given the title *Druzhina*, or 'Bodyguard'. The leading light was the 35-year-old ex-Soviet Lieutenant-Colonel V.V. Gil, a Kuban Cossack and former Chief of Staff of the Red Army's 229th Infantry Division. The *Druzhina*, with only eight German officers and around 1000 Russians volunteers, proved exemplary in combat against the Belorussian partisans. A second group was subsequently formed: *Druzhina* I mustered those considered unsuitable for subversive activities, and *Druzhina* II used the most intelligent and reliable elements for special operations. In March 1942, they were merged under the designation SS-Verband *Druzhina*, or 1st Russian National Brigade, with the motto 'Fight for a New Russia'. Gil adopted the *nom de guerre* 'Rodionov', and was appointed its commanding officer.

The unit stood at about battalion strength, comprising some 3000 men, and was subsequently moved to Nevel, northeast of Polotsk in Belorussia. Here, to help contain a Soviet breakthrough, it was thrown into the frontline almost immediately. HSSPF Belorussia's anti-partisan force was augmented in May 1942 by the inclusion on its strength of SS-Verband *Druzhina*. *Druzhina* was engaged against partisans and it is thought that its size had increased greatly by late 1942, consisting possibly of four battalions and a headquarters. On 18 November 1942, Gil's battalion and the Signalling Battalion formed part of the anti-partisan strength of HSSPF Central Russia. The first defection from a unit which had apparently enjoyed the Germans' confidence occurred during the night of the 24/25 November 1942. After wounding two German workers, killing four others and one SD NCO, 63 men of the 1st company of Gil's battalion went over to the partisans at Kolitschenko. They were wearing SS uniform and carrying all their light and heavy weapons. In the spring of 1943, Gil's men were assigned a defined territory to administer as an autonomous region in the Glubokoe area.

Unreliable indigenous elements

During the summer of 1943, SS-Obergruppenführer Bach-Zelewski launched the largest anti-partisan operation to be held in Belorussia, codenamed 'Cottbus', and under Action Group West *Druzhina* units took part. During this period there was talk of incorporating *Druzhina* into General Vlassov's 'Russian Army of Liberation', and one of Vlassov's senior staff officers, Lieutenant-General Zhilenkov, was moved to Pskov where he was assigned responsibility for forming a '1st Guards Brigade' from among the Russian volunteers. Alarmed by Zhilenkov's arrival and the implied challenge to his authority, Gil determined not only to defect back to the Soviets, but if possible take the brigade with him. On 13 August, in what would appear to have been a prearranged encounter, the 'Zhelezniak Brigade', a strong partisan force, ambushed the brigade and demanded its surrender. Gil then threatened to shoot anyone unwilling to change sides. All the German liaison staff were killed. Despite this, some 30 officers and 500 other ranks refused to go over to the partisans and fought their way out of the encirclement to return to the German lines. Gil's battalion was renamed the 1st Anti-Fascist Brigade and Stalin rewarded him with the Order of the Red Star. During the German anti-partisan operation 'Spring Feast' in April 1944, Gil and the majority of his fellow deserters were killed. The small number who had shown their trustworthiness by fighting their way out of the ambush became, under

Above: The Russian Bronislav Vladislavovich Kaminiski, who raised a private army to fight on behalf of the Germans. This force fought a number of successful actions against partisans in the Bryansk Forest.

Lieutenant-General Zhilenkov's leadership, the First Guards Brigade of the POA (Russian Army of Liberation). Those other members of *Druzhina* who remained loyal to the Germans eventually ended up in the Kaukasischer Waffenverband der SS. The Reichsführer-SS was of course careful to keep the *Druzhina*

fiasco concealed from Hitler, who was merely informed the brigade had been disbanded 'because of indiscipline'.

As 1943 drew to a close, the situation in the East was deteriorating rapidly, and some of the units recruited from the indigenous population in Russia and the Ukraine were beginning to prove unreliable, so it was decided to exchange them for German units in the West. As a result, large numbers of auxiliaries were transported to France, Italy and Yugoslavia, where they fought partisans under SS, police and army command.

No precise estimates of the results of sabotage by Soviet partisans or by the groups and agents in the towns are available. Figures given by partisan commanders were often exaggerated or repeated in reports of several commanders. It was on the basis of such data that Ponomarenko, Chief of the Partisan Movement Central Staff, claimed that during the first two years of the Soviet-German war the partisans of Belorussia alone had killed over 300,000 Germans, caused over 3000 railway accidents and destroyed 3263 bridges, 1191 tanks, 4097 lorries and 895 stores of various kinds. Though

Above: Following partisan attacks, the Germans would invariably instigate retaliatory action. This included the killing of civilians from villages suspected of giving aid to partisans, as above.

these figures are exaggerated, the fact remains that the partisans did have an effect on the German prosecution of the war.

The killings in the East by the SS were so monumental that to look at global figures tends to dehumanise the indescribable horrors perpetrated. By looking at one individual's record it is hoped that the extermination of six million souls is brought into focus. SS-Oberführer Christian Wirth, a former Stuttgart police officer, had been loaned to Operation 'Euthanasia' by SS-Gruppenführer Nebe. Wirth was immediately sent to Poland, under Odilo Globocnik, with the brief to find an efficient method of despatching one million Polish Jews. He selected an area along the Lublin-Lwow railway for his first experimental camp; he went on to head an organisation of a group of four extermination camps.

The inhumanity of Christian Wirth

Wirth decided he wanted nothing to do with gas vans or mobile death units, so instead, a permanent unit of three 'shower rooms' was constructed at the centre of the camp. To further camouflage them, he planted geraniums and kept the surrounding grass cut. The victims were pacified by the thought of a shower, but inside they received the exhaust gas from diesel engines. He had wide doors on both front and back walls to make the removal of gassed victims easier. He was so pleased with the killing centre that he added three more to allow the camp to deal with 1500 Jews daily. A sign was hung over the gate that read, 'Entrance to the Jewish State'. Above the large doors through which the Jews entered the gas chamber was a banner made from a synagogue curtain which stated in Hebrew: 'This is the gate of the Lord into which the righteous shall enter.' Wirth was an egotist without conscience, exemplified by an eyewitness account of when he struck a woman across the face with five lashes of a whip to encourage her into the chamber. The engines failed to work and the victims were crammed in for two hours and 49 minutes before they started. A further 35 minutes passed before all were dead. Then, the workers prised open the victims mouths with iron bars for gold teeth, and searched private parts for hidden valuables. Wirth was dubbed 'the death camp king', but this title aroused the jealousy of others determined to topple him, in particular Höss, who eventually succeeded him. Such was the nature of SS rule in the East.

CHAPTER 9

RED STORM IN THE SOUTH

The second half of 1943 was a time of crises for German forces in the East, which were often only saved from turning into catastrophes by the intervention of Waffen-SS units. By mid-August, for example, a 55km- (34-mile-) wide gap had opened up in the German lines west of Kursk, and Red Army units began to pour through it, threatening Kharkov once again. The *Das Reich* and *Totenkopf* Divisions, together with the *Wiking* Division, were all thrown into battle to prevent the loss of the city, though they were already weakened by the Kursk disaster. *Das Reich* had received all of the *Leibstandarte*'s armour before the latter's transfer to Italy, making it a formidable fighting force. In a reversal of the German capture of Kharkov in March, it was now the Red Army's turn to launch a massive pincer attack, with the 53rd Army driving in from the north and the 57th Army from the south. The 5th Guards Tank Army was to apply the hammer blow. The Russian attack was not quite as effective as the German one, though. The Soviets ran into strong defences, and on just one day of fighting Waffen-SS anti-tank gunners knocked out over 180 Russian tanks. It

Left: A Waffen-SS machine-gun team awaits the next Russian attack during the fighting around Kharkov in August 1943. The SS was instrumental in saving Army Group South.

CHAPTER 10

FIELDS OF GLORY

In northern Russia, 1944 began badly for the Wehrmacht. Having lifted the siege of Leningrad, the Red Army had gone on to the offensive and gradually drove the Germans westwards towards Estonia and Latvia. It was in this sector of the front that most of the west and east European SS volunteer units were concentrated. The main Waffen-SS force in this area was III (Germanisches) SS Panzer Corps, commanded by SS-Gruppenführer Felix Steiner, containing the 11th SS Freiwilligen-Panzergrenadier Division *Nordland* and SS Freiwilligen-Brigade *Nederland*. In these two units alone were volunteers from Norway, Denmark, Holland, France, Finland, Sweden and Switzerland. Allocated to the same sector of the front were the 15th Waffen-Grenadier Division der SS (No 1) and 19th Waffen-Grenadier Division der SS (No 2) from Latvia, 20th Waffen-Grenadier Division der SS (Estnische No 1) from Estonia, the Flemish *Langemarck* Brigade and SS-Sturmbrigade *Wallonien*.

Typical of the foreign volunteers in the Waffen-SS at this time was anti-tank gunner SS-Unterscharführer der Reserve (Flemish Volunteer) Remy Schrynen, *Langemarck* Brigade. He demonstrated his fortitude in many taxing situations. On 2 January 1944, for example, he destroyed three Russian T-34 tanks; on 3 March he was wounded for the seventh time. On the fourth day of the Russian offensive his gun

Left: The strain of battle clearly shows on the faces of these members of III SS Panzer Corps attempting to hold the line at Narva against the Red Army in March 1944.

NO RESPITE

By the spring of 1944 STAVKA, the Soviet High Command, had decided that Belorussia was to be the Red Army's next priority in the north. Stalin intended that the Red Army would drive from its starting point east of Lake Peipus, along a line running through Gorki in the centre, skirting the Pripet Marshes, and on to Odessa on the shores of the Black Sea and push the Germans back some 650km (400 miles) to the very gates of Warsaw itself. For this task he mustered a massive force of 19 armies and two tank armies, with some 1300 aircraft in support.

On the night of 22 June 1944, the main assault began, with the Russians ripping through Army Group Centre. Within just seven days, the entire length of a 320km (200-mile) front stretching from Ostrov on the Lithuanian border to Kovel on the edge of the Pripet Marshes had been completely overrun. In the weeks that followed, some 350,000 German troops were eliminated.

On 25 June 1944 the *Totenkopf* Division was immediately ordered north from Romania to help fend off the Soviet attack west of Minsk. The roads, however, were chaotic, and the division did not reach its destination until 7 July. By then, the Red Army was advancing rapidly towards Grodno, endangering the southern flank of the 4th Army and the northern flank of the battered remnants of the 2nd Army. The *Totenkopf* Division held the line at Grodno for 11 days against massive odds, before being ordered to withdraw towards the southeast to join the mass of German troops retreating slowly towards Warsaw.

Left: The face of the German Army on the Eastern Front in 1944: heavy fatigue due to constant fighting and apprehension about the Red Army's seemingly unstoppable advance

Above: The Germans abandon another Russian town in the face of the Red Army's mid-1944 offensive, which saw the Russians reach the East Prussian border by August 1944. The Eastern Rampart was failing.

In the centre, the Russian westward drive continued. Since 16 July, German counter-attacks had tried in vain to crush the 3rd Belorussian Front's bridgehead over the Niemen, and on 28 July the front advanced from its bridgeheads. By 31 August, when it took Kovno, it had covered 48km (30 miles). On 20 July, the left wing of the 1st Belorussian Front had broken through the German defences near Kovel, crossing the western Bug into Poland.

Zakharov's 2nd Belorussian Front had a more difficult passage, for by mid-July over 10 German divisions had been concentrated on the Grodno-Svisloch line; a defence had been organised and the Germans had begun a number of large- and small-scale counterattacks. However, when Zakharov brought up his reserve army the German force was broken and its reserves swept aside. The armies of the 2nd Belorussian Front surged through Bialystok, and by the end of July stood on the East Prussian border.

These latest defeats convinced the German High Command that the only chance of halting the Russian offensive was to fall back to the line of the Vistula where it might be easier to build a stable defence. An immediate with-drawal began, with the Soviet spearheads hard on the heels of the German rearguards. Lublin fell to the 1st Belorussian Front on 23 July and Brest Litovsk was captured on the 28th.

A sombre occasion was the Soviet liberation of the Nazi death camp at Maidanek, 2km (1.25 miles) west of Lublin, where some 1,500,000 prisoners had been liquidated and the foulest atrocities perpetrated.

While the battle for Brest Litovsk was still in progress, the left wing of the 1st Belorussian

Front was racing towards the Vistula and Warsaw. Between 28 July and 2 August, two bridgeheads were forced across the Vistula south of Warsaw, and throughout August these bridgeheads were the scene of furious battles as the Germans desperately tried to destroy the Soviet footholds on the west bank. The Luftwaffe increased its attacks, and the German ground forces were greatly strengthened by the arrival of two panzer and five infantry divisions during August, as well as four infantry and motorised brigades. The Soviet forces succeeded in holding their bridgeheads with great difficulty, but were not strong enough to extend them and continue the offensive.

Northeast of Warsaw, armoured units of the 1st Belorussian Front had reached the Radzymin-Wolomin area, only to run into stiff German resistance. Here, too, the offensive was halted. A successful defence was followed by a spirited German counterattack by four panzer divisions and one infantry division, which recovered Radzymin and Wolomin, dealt out heavy losses to the Soviet armoured formations, and forced them back 24-32km (15-20 miles) to the south. At last it seemed that the Eastern Front was steady again.

As soon as the first Polish territory was liberated the Committee of National Liberation, led by the Polish Communist Party, became active. Functioning as a provisional government, the Committee had already issued a manifesto entitled *To the Polish People*. This manifesto called on all Poles to fight together

Below: A brief respite for these two Wiking *Division grenadiers allows them to get their bearings, but there is only one way to go – west. The division was pushed back all the way to the River Vistula by August 1944.*

with the Red Army for the freedom and independence of Poland. It also drew up the main features of a programme of radical social change, the building of a new, democratic Poland (troops of the Polish 1st Army were serving in the ranks of the 1st Belorussian Front in the liberation of eastern Poland).

The Red Army begins to stall

As large German reinforcements concentrated on the Vistula Line, resistance stiffened and Soviet problems were increased by serious supply difficulties, particularly in fuel and ammunition, as the Red Army formations had advanced over 480km (300 miles) since 23 June. But the offensive was maintained: all military vehicles were mobilised to get the supplies up to the front, and the civilian population in the liberated areas proffered every possible assistance to the Soviet forces. The Belorussian partisans struck boldly at the German forces, cut their communications, wiped out individual German units, and gave them no chance to blow up bridges or remove valuable materials as they retreated.

When the Red Army reached the approaches to East Prussia and the bank of the Vistula, it had outrun its strength after its sweep through Belorussia. The Soviet troops, already fatigued and considerably weakened in the preceding battles, now had to beat off strong German counterattacks in the Shyaulyay area, east of Warsaw, and in the Magnuszew and Pulawy bridgeheads. By the end of July, it was already clear that the Germans would be able to hold a solid defensive front along the East Prussian approaches and the Narew and Vistula rivers. And now, with the Red Army rapidly approaching the Polish capital, but with the Soviet offensive petering out, the Polish Home Army resistance movement launched the Warsaw Rising. As the Polish Home Army rose up in open revolt on 1 August, the Germans were stunned at the strength of the uprising and initially lost almost two-thirds of the city to the valiant Polish fighters. With the Red Army so near, the Poles believed the city would be taken from the Germans.

What the Poles did not realise was that the Red Army's advance was rapidly running out of steam. Moreover, the Germans were aware of the tired state of the Soviet troops and could concentrate on putting down the uprising. Stalin cynically allowed the Germans to deal with the Poles, as he wanted Poland to be under Soviet occupation after the war. Just to make sure, he refused the Western Allies the use of Soviet air bases from which to launch supply missions, and disassociated the Soviets from what he called the 'Warsaw venture'.

The aim of the rising, as the Polish reactionaries who organised it openly stated at the time, was not to help the Red Army to liberate Poland, but to obstruct it. They considered that by seizing the capital they could establish themselves in power and prevent Stalin's 'people's democratic order' from being established in Poland.

German reorganisation

On 21 July 1944, Hitler ordered General Guderian to take over command of the Eastern Front. His task was to reorganise it and halt the Red Army offensive. The Vistula, with a bridgehead on the east bank at Praga, was adopted as the new line of defence, and Guderian appointed General Vordman to command the sector of the middle Vistula between Jablonna and Deblin. Vordman had commanded the 9th Army which had been almost obliterated in Belorussia in June. The 2nd Army was to concentrate along the lower reaches of the Bug, north of the 9th Army.

As this regrouping was taking place, but before the new defensive measures could become effective, the frontline was nearing the Vistula, and all the while the German evacuation from Warsaw was being accelerated. Between 21 and 25 July, German stores, workshops, civilian institutions and military command alike left Warsaw. Police and army units were also pulling out.

Then, on 26 July, the directives of the new commander of the German front began to take effect. German administrative authorities and the police returned to Warsaw. On 27 July,

Luftwaffe General Stahel took over military command of Warsaw. German civilian authorities announced that the city would be defended against the Red Army, and called upon the Polish population of the capital to cooperate; through the street public address system and wall posters they commanded that 100,00 men come forward to put up fortifications round the city. Guards at German institutions were strengthened, assault guns were placed at main street intersections, and police and tank patrols in the city were increased. Units of the German 73rd Infantry Division began arriving on the outskirts of Warsaw.

During the night of 28 July and on the days that followed, Warsaw could hear the sound of the battle being fought for the town of Wolomin between the German XXXIX Panzer

Above: A brief rest for these Germans on the Eastern Front in mid-1944 as they pull back in the face of Russian pressure. For Hitler and his Third Reich it was a moment of crisis, but the Waffen-SS would come to the rescue.

Corps and the Soviet 2nd Tank Army. On 21 July 1944, the Communist National Council set up a Committee of National Liberation, which it intended to foist upon the country as a political authority. When, on 23 July, Moscow radio published a manifesto to the Polish nation issued by this committee, it described the Polish Government in London and its organs in Poland as usurpers.

These moves seemed to indicate that the Soviet Union was going to try to impose its will upon Poland through this Committee of

National Liberation, without regard to the Polish Government in London. On 30 July, the Polish Prime Minister Stanislaw Mikolajczyk arrived in Moscow from London. On 31 July, he had his first conversation with Soviet Foreign Secretary, Molotov, on how to coordinate the campaign against the Germans in Poland.

The Polish insurgents

The commander-in-chief of the Home Army, General Tadeusz Komorowski (codenamed Bor), had decided that the Home Army would, at an opportune moment, attack the German troops in Warsaw. This would shorten the fight for control of the city and minimise losses, and in any case would enable the Home Army to meet the entering Red Army as hosts and masters in their own city.

General Bor estimated that a rapid capture of Warsaw was in Soviet interests, both politically, since it was the capital, and militarily, since it was the largest and most convenient communications centre on the Vistula from which to launch a further advance west. On 25 July, General Bor obtained the agreement of the London Poles to engage in a battle for Warsaw and presented this decision to the presidium of the Polish underground parliament, and duly obtained its agreement. Bor informed the Commander of the Warsaw District, Colonel Antoni Chrusciel (codenamed Monter), and gave the order to get the district ready for action. The action was to follow the plan of the general uprising, for which the units of the district had been preparing for three years.

The Poles faced an opponent about equal numerically, but overwhelmingly superior in armament and technical facilities, who could also call upon air and armoured support, neither of which the Home Army possessed.

The numerical strength of Home Army units in Warsaw was approximately 38,000 soldiers, of which about 4000 were women. Units of the Home Army belonging to the Warsaw District and based in the vicinity of the capital numbered approximately 11,000. These forces and their chain of command were organised in seven urban and one suburban precincts,

which in their turn were subdivided into sectors. The armament consisted of heavy and light infantry weapons and was sufficient for 25 per cent of the effectives, and there was enough ammunition for seven days of fighting. Deficiencies were to be supplemented by captured weapons from Germans, and supplies of arms were also expected from the west, through the usual aerial drops which had been going on for the last three years.

Besides the units mentioned, there were two organisations in Warsaw not subordinated to the Home Army. They were *Narodowe Sily Zbrojne* (NSZ), or the National Armed Forces, a right-wing, nationalist federation; and *Armia Ludowa* (AL), the People's Army, a Communist organisation wholly subordinate to Moscow. Each movement had a few hundred men in the city, and their units later joined the fight at the side of the Home Army.

The Warsaw Uprising begins

The numerical strength of the German garrison was estimated by the Home Army at about 40,000. Some units had been pulled out between 21 and 25 July, but every day other units were being quartered in or near the capital, and there were reasons to believe that numerically the Polish and German sides were evenly matched. On 31 July, at the afternoon briefing of the commanders of the Home Army, Colonel Monter, Commander of the Warsaw District, reported that the German bridgehead on the east bank of the Vistula had been breached by Soviet armour and that its defence had been disorganised. According to the report, Soviet detachments had taken the suburban localities of Radosc, Milosna, Okuniew, and Radzymin.

On the basis of this report, in the presence of Deputy Prime Minister Jankowski, General Bor ordered Colonel Monter to attack the Germans on the following day, 1 August at 1700 hours. On the very same day, at 1830 hours, Colonel Monter issued his orders to the units under his command, though some of them did not receive them until the following morning, as the police curfew delayed their transmission.

Above: German troops in a Polish town in July 1944. The Russian 1944 summer offensive saw the Red Army advance 730km (450 miles) in five weeks, though it then began to outrun its supply lines.

The military situation round the German bridgehead that day was as follows: Soviet armoured detachments did make a breach in the southern perimeter of the bridgehead, even capturing the general commanding the German 73rd Infantry Division, but the German defence had not been disorganised and they were not forced to retreat from the east bank of the Vistula. At the same time, a battle between German and Soviet armour was being fought round Siedlce, farther east, and its outcome was not yet clear.

The concentration of Home Army units at their assembly points was carried out in the afternoon of 1 August without German counter action, although owing to the secrecy needed only 85 per cent of the troops managed to reach their appointed places.

At 1700 hours, Home Army units launched their attacks at prearranged objectives. Within minutes the entire city was engulfed in fighting, German patrols and troops in the streets were attacked and disarmed, and many objectives, those which were not powerfully reinforced or strongly manned, were captured. Those which were properly manned, however, managed to repulse Home Army assaults. Where the initial attacks were not successful, they were renewed during the night, many of them several times, and those parts of the city cleared of the Germans were occupied by the Home Army.

Throughout 2-3 August, the Home Army renewed its general assault on German strongpoints not taken on the first day, but it was not particularly successful for it lacked the heavy assault weapons necessary to reduce pillboxes and other reinforced concrete defences.

Both sides suffered heavy casualties in killed and wounded. The Poles captured a con-

siderable quantity of both weapons and ammunition, but German resistance, though largely uncoordinated at the outset, proved very strong almost everywhere.

The intensity of the fighting exacted its toll, and on the Polish side ammunition ran low despite the quantities captured. This, combined with the mounting casualties and disappointing outcome of the attacks on 2 and 3 August, dampened the momentum of Home Army offensive operations.

Bach-Zelewski takes control

Then, to the disappointment of all, the sounds of the battle waging on the east bank of the Vistula between German and Soviet forces, which up until then had been steadily gaining in intensity, grew fainter on 3 August, to be followed the next day by complete silence. In addition, the Red Air Force disappeared from the sky above Warsaw on 2 August.

Having considered all these factors and after consulting Bor, Colonel Monter ordered his troops to abandon their offensive tasks and to switch to defence as from 5 August. At the conclusion of this initial stage of the fighting, the Home Army controlled three-fifths of the Warsaw itself.

Documents captured by the Germans over the previous years had already given them a fragmentary idea of the plan for general uprising planned by the Home Army. Judging by the behaviour and attitude of the Polish population, they counted on the possibility of a Polish attack in the last days of July, but they believed that such an attack would take place at night.

When reports of the fighting reached Hitler and Himmler, their reaction was instantaneous. On 2 August 1944, Hitler appointed a new commander for units engaged against the Polish rising, SS-Obergruppenführer und General der Waffen-SS und Polizei Erich von

Left: A Tiger tank of the **Wiking** *Division outside Warsaw in August 1944. The division was part of IV SS Panzer Corps, which threw the Red Army back just before the city in August, stabilising the front temporarily.*

men laid down their weapons. Thus ended an epic and heroic uprising.

At the same time as the operations against Mokotow and Zoliborz, the Germans set out to dislodge the Home Army from the Forest of Kampinos. These troops, two infantry regiments and two cavalry squadrons, about 2500 men in all, were commanded by Major A. Kotowski. They acted in an auxiliary capacity in the uprising, receiving aerial drops from the West, transporting them to Zoliborz, and generally harassing German communications from the rear.

A special group detached from the German 9th Army, designated Sterschuppe, began operations against the forest on 27 September. Major Kotowski had recognised the German build-up and moved his troops to the southern edge of the forest, intending to break out to the south. The German attack thus missed its target, and met only rearguard units. Major Kotowski's column moved south from the forest until it came upon the Skierniewice-Zyrandow railway line, where at noon on 29 September an armoured train barred its way. Detachments of German tanks then caught up with it and dispersed it, but only one cavalry squadron, about 100 troopers managed to fight its way through to Kielce province.

The last pockets of resistance

Towards the end of September the situation of the insurgents was becoming more critical with every day that passed. They had lost control of the river bank, the outlying bastions of Mokotow and Zoliborz had fallen, and the Forest of Kampinos was in German hands. Ammunition was running out, insufficient water was being drawn from improvised wells, and they were short of medical supplies. From 20 September onwards barley and sugar were their only sustenance. The troops had no warm clothing, and instances of soldiers fainting at barricades from exhaustion were becoming more frequent.

After consultations with the civilian Resistance leaders, the Home Army Headquarters, accepted that to continue fighting would not bring the aims of the uprising any nearer, though it would prolong the suffering and losses of the population. SS-Obergruppenführer und General der Waffen-SS und Polizei Erich von dem Bach-Zelewski's invitation to enter into negotiations made through the Polish Red Cross was therefore accepted. A general ceasefire was agreed on 2 October, and on that day a Polish delegation signed an act of surrender at the German headquarters at Ozarow.

To the victor the spoils

After more than two months of fighting the Polish troops laid down their arms. The Germans evacuated the entire remaining population of the city and proceeded to systematically destroy whatever was left standing. Any moveables worth taking were shipped to the Reich. It is impossible to arrive at an estimate of civilian losses with any accuracy, but the figure of 150,00 may be close to reality. German losses, according to Bach-Zelewski, amounted to 26,000.

As with the earlier revolts, Himmler wished to see this fight as a battle honour for the SS, so the Warsaw Shield was instituted on 10 December 1944 and was intended to be awarded 'as a battle badge to members of the Armed Forces and non-military personnel who between 1 August and 2 October 1944 were honourably engaged in the fighting in Warsaw'. The award was to have been made by the commander Bach-Zelewski, but the factory producing the awards was bombed out, and so none were issued.

Outside Warsaw, the *Totenkopf* Division was unable to rapidly make good its losses, whereas the Soviets were back up to strength and ready to launch yet another attack against the city by 10 October. This time the weakened Germans were forced back to the northwest of the city, but managed to stabilise their positions quickly and halt the Soviets once again.

By the end of October 1944, Romania and Bulgaria had capitulated and defected to the Soviets, while in the north Finland had sued for peace. The Red Army's 1st Baltic Front had retaken Memel in Lithuania on 10 October, while Yeremenko's 2nd Baltic Front had captured Riga, the Latvian capital. The Russian offensive had cut off two entire German armies in Courland, comprising some 33 divisions. Rather than tie up a considerable number of troops in trying to eliminate them, STAVKA chose an air and sea blockade of the pocket.

Among the units able to escape by sea were the remaining Dutch SS volunteers from the *Nederland* Brigade. The ship evacuating them was attacked and sunk, but some of the Dutch SS men did survive and formed the nucleus of the 23rd Freiwilligen-Panzergrenadier Division *Nederland*. The unit went back into action at Stargard in Pommerania and also saw action at Stettin, before being forced back towards Berlin itself.

A weakened Army Group Centre

In January 1945 the Red Army was ordered to drive the Germans out of Poland. Marshal Zhukov and his 1st Belorussian Front was to drive to Poznan, while Marshal Koniev would direct his assault towards Breslau to the south. Each massive force comprised over one million men, with over 30,000 guns and 7000 tanks between them. Opposing them was a weakened Army Group Centre with 400,000 men and just over 1000 tanks. That said, the Germans still had some 580,000 troops in East Prussia.

On 12 January Koniev's attack began after a massive artillery barrage lasting 105 minutes. Two days later Zhukov's forces joined in the assault, his forces aiding the Soviet-formed 1st Polish Army in taking Warsaw. During the second half of January the Red Army seized Silesia, one of Germany's most important industrial regions, rich in coal deposits, and by early February had reached the River Oder. Those German strongpoints, such as Breslau, which had withstood the Soviet onslaught were merely bypassed, to be dealt with later.

All along the front, the Waffen-SS divisions were being destroyed by the Russian offensive. By the spring of 1945, most of them were carrying out a spirited fighting withdrawal through Hungary and into Austria. The *Wiking*

Above: The Warsaw Shield commemorating those who 'were honourably engaged in the fighting in Warsaw'. Ironically, it was never issued as the factory producing the awards was destroyed in an Allied bombing raid.

Division was all but destroyed in the fighting for the approaches to Vienna. In the central and northern sectors of the Eastern Front, those Waffen-SS units still in action were principally east and west European volunteer formations. The level of determination shown by these volunteers in their attempts to hold the Soviet advance was quite exceptional, if not entirely surprising. Those units raised from eastern European states no longer had any homelands to return to as their nations had been conquered by the Russians and were now in Stalin's iron grip. The only option was to try and reach the Western Allies in order to surrender. Those who surrendered to the Soviets were usually shot out of hand.

THE BLACK GUARD DIES

From August 1944, as the Red Army drove through Romania and Bulgaria, Hitler's east European allies deserted him. As Army Groups E and F, under Field Marshal von Weichs, were forced back through Yugoslavia, the ethnic volunteer 7th SS Freiwilligen-Gebirgs Division *Prinz Eugen* was decimated south of Vukovar in January 1945, and the survivors withdrew into Austria.

In Hungary, the capital Budapest came under the protection of General Otto Wöhler's Army Group South. Units committed to the defence of the city included the 8th SS Kavallerie Division *Florian Geyer*, 22nd Freiwilligen-Kavallerie Division der SS *Maria Theresia* and 18th SS Freiwilligen-Panzergrenadier Division *Horst Wessel*, although some of the latter's units were sent to Galicia and others helped suppress the Slovak Uprising during August-October 1944.

In October 1944 the Red Army crossed the Hungarian border and raced for the Danube, reaching the river to the south of Budapest and establishing a bridgehead on the west bank, from where it could launch future operations.

To the southwest of the city lay Lake Balaton, between which and the area around Budapest the Germans had established strong defensive positions. By 20 December 1944 the Soviets had advanced across the Danube and reached the southern shore of Lake Balaton.

Left: A fine study of a Panther and grenadiers of IV SS Panzer Corps in January 1945. The corps attempted to relieve Budapest, but the city fell to the Russians in February 1945.

The main German defences, however, proved a difficult nut for the Red Army to crack, as by this stage of the war the Germans were making use of natural defence lines, such as rivers, and 'fortress cities'. The Soviets had also over-stretched their supply lines. The breathing space for the Germans was short, though. Marshal Tolbukhin diverted his attack past the east of Budapest, and with the 6th Guards Tank Army attacking from the northeast and the 46th Army from the south, the city was eventually surrounded in a massive Russian pincer action. Fighting raged for sometime, the Soviets unable to rout the Germans and the latter unable to throw back the attackers.

Budapest falls

On 26 December 1944, IV SS Panzer Corps, comprising the 3rd SS Panzer Division *Totenkopf* and the 5th SS Panzer Division *Wiking*, were transferred from the Warsaw area in an attempt to relieve Budapest. Two attempts to raise the siege of the city were beaten back by the Soviets, before they in turn launched a counterattack which forced IV SS Panzer Corps on to the defensive. The beleaguered garrison struggled on, but the odds had been impossible. After two weeks of fighting, the relief attempt had to be called off. The garrison, weakened and forced into a small area, attempted a breakout on 11 February 1945, when some 30,000 of the troops inside the city tried to force a way to the west. But the retreating Germans were cut to pieces: the 8th SS Kavallerie Division *Florian Geyer* and 22nd Freiwilligen-Kavallerie Division der SS *Maria Theresia* were annihilated, and only 800 of the survivors broke the encirclement and reached the safety of the German lines. Among them were 170 troops of the Waffen-SS, all that remained of the 8th and 22nd Kavallerie Divisions. *Florian Geyer*'s youthful comman-

Left: Mud massively affected the war on the Eastern Front. It totally destroyed mobility, as the 6th SS Panzer Army found to its cost at the beginning of Operation 'Spring Awakening' in March 1945.

der, SS-Brigadeführer und Generalmajor der Waffen-SS Joachim Rumohr, committed suicide after being wounded while attempting to escape from the Hungarian capital. Budapest surrendered on 12 February.

The survivors of the two SS cavalry divisions formed the nucleus of a new unit – 37th SS Freiwilligen-Kavallerie Division *Lützow* – but it never reached the strength of one regiment, and existed for only three months before being swallowed up in the Russian advance.

The fall of Budapest released a large number of Russian troops for a fresh offensive against the Third Reich, which threatened the German-held oilfields at Nagykanizsa, Hungary. Hitler was horrified at the thought of losing this precious source of oil, and decided that only a new offensive could throw the Red Army back over the Danube and save the overall situation in Hungary.

General Wöhler's Army Group South, comprising the 6th SS Panzer Army, 8th Army, 6th Army and the Hungarian 3rd Army, would strike south from the Margarethe defence lines, while Army Group Southeast's 2nd Army would attack from the west of the Soviet lines. This pincer movement, it was hoped, would crush Tolbukhin's 3rd Ukrainian Front, made up of the 4th Guards Army, 26th Army, 57th Army and 1st Bulgarian Army. IV SS Panzer Corps would remain around Lake Balaton.

The 6th SS Panzer Army

Led by SS-Oberstgruppenführer 'Sepp' Dietrich, the 6th SS Panzer Army consisted of the finest Waffen-SS formations: the *Leibstandarte* Division, *Das Reich* Division, 9th SS Panzer Division *Hohenstaufen* and 12th SS Panzer Division *Hitlerjugend*. The *Leibstandarte* Division, led by SS-Brigadeführer Otto Kumm, and the 12th SS Panzer Division *Hitlerjugend*, commanded by SS-Oberführer Hugo Kraas, were grouped together as I SS Panzer Corps, while the *Das Reich* Division, temporarily commanded by SS-Standartenführer Rudolf Lehmann, and the 9th SS Panzer Division *Hohenstaufen*, led by SS-Oberführer Sylvester Stadler, formed II SS Panzer Corps.

The operation was codenamed 'Spring Awakening', but the omens for success were not good. The area around Lake Balaton is predominantly marshy, although under normal circumstances the severe frosts during the early part of the year render the ground hard enough to bear the weight of heavy vehicles. However, in the spring of 1945 the thaw came much earlier than expected, and the terrain was turned into a sea of mud, into which 'Sepp' Dietrich's panzers sank up to their turrets in some extreme instances.

A poor start to 'Spring Awakening'

As a preliminary to the main attack, I SS Panzer Corps had smashed the Soviet bridgehead around Estergom with little difficulty. Once the Soviets became aware of a large body of élite Waffen-SS troops in the region, however, they quickly realised that a major offensive was imminent, and began to strengthen their defences, increasing the depth of their minefields and preparing anti-tank defences. This prelude to the main attack, though successful in its own right, had merely forewarned the Red Army of what was to come.

On 6 March, the day the operation commenced, heavy snow had made conditions even worse. I SS Panzer Corps was best placed for the attack, the men having reached their positions in time, but II SS Panzer Corps was still floundering in the mud, its heavy vehicles finding the going almost impossible. Not surprisingly, the German attack began to suffer heavy losses almost from the start. However, the Waffen-SS soldiers threw themselves into the attack with fanatical bravery, driving the enemy back, in the case of I SS Panzer Corps for distances of up to 40km (25 miles). II SS Panzer Corps, however, could only manage an advance of around 8km (five miles) at best.

As always, the Soviets could make good their losses relatively quickly, while the Germans could only call upon men who were often poorly trained and equipped, and had no motivation to sacrifice their lives at this late stage in the war. The offensive slowed, and German aircraft began to spot evidence of a massive Soviet build-up, obviously intended for a counterattack.

The Soviet offensive began on 16 March along the entire sector west of Budapest. The Russian sledgehammer blow stopped the German offensive in its tracks. Dietrich desperately reshuffled his forces to reinforce the areas under threat, but when he did so the Soviets soon swamped the areas from which the reinforcements had been taken. The 6th SS Panzer Army was in danger of being cut off, as IV SS Panzer Corps struggled to maintain the German base line. *Das Reich* desperately battled to hold open a corridor of escape for its comrades, but the defection of the Hungarian Army left the flank of II SS Panzer Corps wide open to the Soviets. The Germans had no option but to retreat or lose the best remaining divisions they still possessed on the Eastern Front. By 25 March, the Russians had torn a 100km (62-mile) gap in the German defences.

As well as the four élite panzer divisions of the 6th Panzer Army, and the two panzer divisions of IV SS Panzer Corps, the 16th SS Panzergrenadier Division *Reichsführer-SS* and 18th SS Freiwilligen-Panzergrenadier Division *Horst Wessel*, were also committed to battle around Lake Balaton. *Horst Wessel* had been fortunate enough to escape the encirclement of Budapest and had retreated into Slovakia. Within 10 days of the offensive being launched, however, it had been totally wiped out.

The Waffen-SS in disgrace

Hitler was infuriated by the failure of his Waffen-SS divisions. When the news of the near annihilation of 'Sepp' Dietrich's units – the *Leibstandarte*, *Das Reich*, *Totenkopf* and *Hohenstaufen* Divisions – reached him, he erupted in wild fury. Realising that his order to hold Vienna had been disobeyed, he was horrified that his crack SS units, although completely exhausted and their will to fight diminished, had taken refuge in the city. Hitler cancelled all promotions given on his birthday, 20 April 1945, and ordered that all the surviving members of those units must remove their prized cuff titles. Himmler, who did not have

Above: Waffen-SS soldiers in Poland at the beginning of 1945. By this time the Russians had a superiority of 15 to one on the Eastern Front. It was only the Red Army's over-stretched supply lines which constrained it.

the courage to face his commanders with such an order in person, transmitted it to them in writing instead. On hearing the order, Dietrich summoned the four commanders of those units – Otto Kumm, Karl Kreutz, Hellmuth Becker and Sylvester Stadler – to a conference at his headquarters in Vienna, where he stated categorically that not a cuff title was to be removed, and retorted to his commanders: 'There's your reward for all that you have done these past five years.' He sent a stiff reply to Hitler's headquarters refusing to implement the order. Another story relates that at the same time he packed up his own decorations in a chamber pot and sent them off to Hitler with his reply. Whether this story is true is unknown, but it illustrates Dietrich's feelings. Despite the wrath of Hitler, the professionalism of the Waffen-SS was such that its units continued to fight for him and Germany until the end.

After smashing the German offensive around Lake Balaton, the Soviet advance continued to the west of Budapest in a two-pronged movement towards Pápa and Györ. By 2 April the Red Army had reached the Neusiedler Lake, on the border between Hungary and Austria, and two days later the last German soldiers had been thrown out of Hungary. The Soviet 46th Army was then transported by boat along the Danube to attack Vienna from the north, while the 4th Guards

Army drove towards the city from the south-east. Of the Waffen-SS divisions which had fought in Hungary, most had withdrawn into Austria to defend Vienna.

The 9th SS Panzer Division *Hohenstaufen* had been badly mauled in Hungary, so its remnants were formed into small battle groups, which fought dogged a rearguard action during the withdrawal towards Vienna. The 3rd SS Panzer Division *Totenkopf* also fought in defence of the Austrian capital, while the 12th SS Panzer Division *Hitlerjugend* withdrew into strong defensive positions in the mountainous area around Wienerwald, to the southwest of the city, but was then forced out of its positions by the unrelenting Soviet pressure after only a few days.

The fall of Vienna

The *Das Reich* Division put up a stubborn defence to the south of Vienna, before withdrawing into the city itself and becoming involved in bitter fighting around the Florisdorf Bridge on 13 and 14 April. Despite its efforts, it was gradually driven out of the city by intense Russian pressure. Elements continued to fight in the area to the west of Vienna, but the bulk of the division's remnants were sent to the region east of Dresden to help in the futile attempt to hold back Soviet units swarming into Germany itself. The fall of Vienna on 13 April 1945 netted the Soviets over 125,00 prisoners. To the north, the *Der Führer* Regiment was fighting an insurgency in Prague from 6 to 8 May. In its westward retreat from that city, it transported as many of the German population as possible out of Russian hands. However, rather than pursue the retreating Germans, Stalin halted major operations in Austria to concentrate on the push on Berlin.

As the battered German armies on the Eastern Front retreated deep into the Reich,

Left: Inspector of the Wehretüghtigungslarger (Special Military Preparatory Schools) Gerhard Hein, holder of the Knight's Cross with Oakleaves, instructs **Hitlerjugend** *recruits in the dying months of the war.*

the Waffen-SS divisions were once again to play a major role as rearguard units. The 10th SS Panzer Division *Frundsberg*, serving in Pomerania as part of SS-Obergruppenführer Felix Steiner's 11th Panzer Army in early 1945, took part in an attack on Zhukov's 1st Belorussian Front as it advanced on Berlin. On 16 February, *Frundsberg*, *Nordland*, *Nederland* and *Wallonien* attacked in a southwesterly direction, smashing into Zhukov's northern flank. The weakened German divisions, however, did not have the strength to seriously deflect the massive Soviet assault, and were driven back within a couple of days.

The advance to Berlin

The Russians now took breath for the final push, the capture of Berlin. In the north was Rokossovsky with the 2nd Belorussian Front, in the centre Zhukov with the 1st Belorussian Front, and in the south Koniev with the 1st Ukrainian Front. For the Red Army commanders it was to be a race to see who could reach the Reich's capital first. This rivalry was encouraged by Stalin, who used it to get most out of his commanders. On 28 March 1945, Zhukov had established a bridgehead over the Oder at Küstrin, where he would launch his attack. Wishing to achieve maximum impact, he decided to open his attack with an artillery barrage of unparalleled ferocity, employing over 8000 artillery pieces in a 30-minute barrage. This would be followed by an immediate and massive assault. Zhukov had nearly 150 searchlights brought up to the launch point, intending to bounce their powerful beams off the low cloud cover and blind the German defenders. Koniev, on the other hand, was taking no chances, and intended a prolonged barrage of some 145 minutes, followed by an attack under cover of darkness.

The first probing attacks began on 14 April, and two days latter the main assault began. But the German defenders were aware of Zhukov's plan and withdrew from their positions before the artillery barrage began. Once it had ended, they quickly returned to their positions and were waiting for the Soviet assault troops. The searchlight tactic did not work, as they illuminated the attacking Soviets, making them ideal targets. Despite Zhukov's threats, his troops could not throw the Germans out of their strongly defended positions on the Seelow Heights opposite his bridgehead. Instead of the immediate victory he had expected, three full days of the most bitter fighting were required before the Germans could be slowly forced back. By 19 April, though, the German defences had been overrun, the Seelow Heights captured and Rokossovsky's push from the north launched.

Koniev ordered his 3rd and 4th Guards Tank Armies to break into the city on 20 April, but three days later Stalin had declared that it was to be Zhukov's troops who would make the main assault. Zhukov's men would have the honour of capturing the Führer's bunker and the Reichstag itself. Hitler is said to have inspected some survivors of the 10th SS Panzer Division *Frundsberg* at the bunker on 20 April, and the conditions surrounding the Nazi inner circle had by now become farcical.

The Battle of Berlin

On 21 April Hitler had ordered an attack to relieve the city. General Theodor Busse, defending the Oder Line with his 9th Army to the southeast of Berlin, was to march to the relief of the city. To the west, General Walther Wenck, holding back the Americans, was to do the same, and Steiner's 11th Panzer Army was to launch an attack from the north to relieve Berlin. But it was all fantasy. If Busse and Wenck had abandoned their positions to relieve the city, their pitifully few troops would have been instantly overwhelmed. As for Steiner, his 'panzer army' existed on paper only, as his best troops had already been sacrificed or sent into the city. *Nordland* had been sent into Berlin, *Nederland* was sent south to contain a Soviet attack, and the Walloons had been cut to pieces.

By 25 April Berlin was completely surrounded, and the next day 500,000 Red Army troops swarmed into the city itself. The battle for the city was savage, and the Waffen-SS took part in

this last battle. On 28 April, the Soviets broke through the inner city defences and stormed towards the Reichstag. As usual, the SS fought with great courage. The battered buildings had been turned into a fortress, with heavy machine guns and artillery emplaced behind makeshift gun ports.

The SS Begleit-Kommando was the unit charged with Hitler's protection, and it was the SS who had the task of disposing of the Führer's remains. In the closing days of the war, Hitler had informed SS-Sturmbannführer Otto Günsche that he and Eva Braun were going to commit suicide. Furthermore, he was to be sure that he burned their bodies so that they did not fall into Russian hands. 'I don't

Above: Waffen-SS soldiers fighting in Austria in March 1945. Both the Hohenstaufen *and* Totenkopf *Divisions fought in the defence of Vienna in April, but were unable to prevent the city falling to the Russians on the 13th.*

want to be put on display in some Russian wax-works'. he informed Günsche.

Hitler committed suicide on 30 April 1945, and Günsche was the first person to see his body. He ordered SS-Sturmbannführer Erich Kempka to forage for the fuel necessary to incinerate the corpses. Eva Braun was laid next to Hitler and the corpses ignited by Bormann in a Viking-funeral pyre, in accordance with Hitler's last orders. SS-Oberführer

Wilhelm Mohnke wept openly when Hitler committed suicide, and he set fire to the bunker on the following day, 1 May. He joined one of the escape groups on that night, only to be captured later by the Russians while hiding in a cellar in the Schönhauser Allee.

The first Soviet assault on the Reichstag on 30 April was supported by artillery and Katyusha rocket launchers. Three battalions of infantry charged forward in the face of heavy fire and managed to breach the defences. Inside the building, the fighting degenerated into hand-to-hand combat. The SS had turned the cellar into a fortress, and it took two days of heavy fighting before they were defeated. Some 2500 of the Reichstag's defenders were killed, with another 2600 taken prisoner. By that time Hitler was dead and the battle for Berlin was over. At 1500 hours on 2 May, Lieutenant-General Weidling surrendered the city to the Russians. There were still groups of Waffen-SS troops fighting in various pockets of

Above: The remains of a German town near Berlin, April 1945. By this stage of the war the élite divisions of the Waffen-SS were shadows of their former selves, but they continued to put up a spirited fight.

Right: Volkssturm ('Home Guard') recruits receive instruction in the use of the MG 42 machine gun in Berlin, April 1945. Such measures were wholly inadequate to resist the might of the advancing Red Army.

the shrinking Reich, and they continued to fight until all the formal surrender negotiations had been completed.

The price the Waffen-SS paid in the East is illustrated by how it soldiers entered captivity. Their mode of surrender was not one of subjugation, but pride in their position as Hitler's élite. The 2nd SS Panzer Division *Das Reich*, in the last days of the war, was able to retreat to the west and into American captivity. The 3rd

SS Panzer Division *Totenkopf* had withdrawn to the northwest of Vienna and surrendered to the Americans on 9 May. But its members were then handed over to the Russians, and few of the Waffen-SS soldiers survived Russian captivity. The 4th *SS-Polizei* Panzergrenadier Division, after a brief rest southwest of Stettin, fought its way from an area north of Berlin, across the Elbe to Wittenberge-Lenzen and into American captivity.

Having fought a defensive action from Stuhlweissenburg west of Budapest back into Czechoslovakia, the men of the 5th SS Panzer Division *Wiking* were released from their oaths by the commander, SS-Oberführer Ullrich. He gave his officers the choice of remaining with the men, or of striking out for home. Such was the unit's discipline that it surrendered to the Americans whole on 13 May.

Above: Volkssturm learn how to use the Panzerschreck anti-tank weapon in Berlin in the last days of the war. Up until the end Himmler's Escort Battalion scoured the city's streets, hanging deserters and 'shirkers'.

The pathetic remnants of the 9th SS Panzer Division *Hohenstaufen* surrendered to the Americans at Seyr in Austria, as did the *Leibstandarte* Division. The 10th SS Panzer Division *Frundsberg* was under the 4th Armoured Army, Army Group Centre, in May, fighting near Cottbus and farther south in Saxony. The division moved to the Protectorate of Bohemia and Moravia under Army Group Centre, and entered Russian captivity at Schönau. The 12th SS Panzer Division *Hitlerjugend* managed to surrender to the Americans on 8 May, it they crossed the demarcation line near the town of Enns, southeast of Linz, and entered American captivity. Just before crossing the demarcation line, and at less than 1.6km (one mile) from it, SS-Brigadeführer und Generalmajor der Waffen-SS Hugo Kraas inspected the remnants of his division in one last review. Only 455 men and one tank were all that remained of what had been one of German's foremost armoured divisions. Proud and stubborn even in defeat, they had refused to comply with the American order that their vehicles should be draped with white flags as a token of surrender.

The end of the supermen

The 11th SS Freiwilligen-Panzergrenadier Division *Nordland* was smashed in the Battle of Berlin. The 14th Waffen Grenadier Division der SS (ukrainische No 1) from the Ukraine surrendered to the Soviets in Czechoslovakia, and the bulk of its surviving personnel were promptly shot. Part of the 15th Waffen-Grenadier Division der SS (lettische No 1) from Latvia participated in the defence of Berlin. The 16th SS Panzergrenadier Division *Reichsführer-SS* withdrew into Unterstelermark in the south of Austria, but became fragmented. Some units of the 16th SS Panzergrenadier Division *Reichsführer-SS* surrendered south of the River Drau, while others withdrew towards Klagenfurt and surrendered to the Americans and British.

The 22nd Freiwilligen-Kavallerie Division der SS *Maria Theresia*, which was predominantly Hungarian, was destroyed in the fighting for Budapest. The Red Army also overran the predominantly Hungarian volunteer 25th Waffen-Grenadier Division der SS (ungarische No 1) *Hunyadi* and 26th Waffen-Grenadier Division der SS (ungarische No 2) *Hungaria*, while they were still forming. The 34th Waffen-Grenadier Division der SS *Landstorm Nederland*, little more than a regiment, was wiped out in the fall of Berlin, and the motley remnants of both the 27th SS Freiwilligen-Panzergrenadier Division (flämische No 1) *Langemarck* and the 28th SS Freiwilligen-Panzergrenadier Division *Wallonien* were also wiped out during the fighting for the Reich's capital, as were the remaining volunteers of the French 33rd Waffen-Grenadier Division der SS (französische No 1) *Charlemagne*.

On the day after the capitulation, 13 French volunteers were shot without the benefit of a court martial near Bad Reichenhall. The order for the execution was given by the French General Leclerc, commander of the French 2nd Armoured Division, despite the fact that these French volunteers were wearing German uniform. They had only been deployed in their units in the East, and had surrendered to the Americans on the day of capitulation. These unfortunate volunteers were then handed over by the US Army to the support Leclerc Division. The general took a personal interest in these French prisoners of war and asked them, 'why are you wearing those German uniforms?' One prisoner replied, 'General, why are you wearing an American uniform?', and that was enough to sign their death warrants.

The final reckoning

The Waffen-SS had failed to bring the Führer victory, but it had fought with courage and tenacity throughout, although it is impossible to neglect the appalling atrocities committed in Russia. The actions of Waffen-SS soldiers without doubt lengthened the war in the East, but by how much is very hard to quantify. Possibly their tenacity gave a false sense of security not only to Hitler and Himmler, but also to the German High Command. Without them, the attempts to sue for peace by the officer corps might have been prosecuted more diligently, and the attempt on Hitler's life on 20 July 1944 might well have born greater fruits, but in the event, it gave greater control to the SS. The terrible loss of life both on the battlefield and in the extermination camps might well have been alleviated somewhat.

The Waffen-SS was an organisation that had fought in a manner never encountered before. And was to lay the foundation for the integrated NATO defences after the war. But if its military exploits were exemplary, its ideological beliefs still leave a bad taste in the mouth.

1ST SS PANZER DIVISION *LEIBSTANDARTE SS ADOLF HITLER*
SS-Panzergrenadier Regiment 1
SS-Panzergrenadier Regiment 2
SS-Panzer Regiment 1
SS-Panzer Artillerie Regiment

2ND SS PANZER DIVISION *DAS REICH*
SS-Panzergrenadier Regiment 3 *Deutschland*
SS-Panzergrenadier Regiment 4 *Der Führer*
SS-Panzer Regiment 2
SS-Panzer Artillerie Regiment 2

3RD SS PANZER DIVISION *TOTENKOPF*
SS-Panzergrenadier Regiment 5 *Thule*
SS-Panzergrenadier Regiment 6 *Theodor Eicke*
SS-Panzer Regiment 3
SS-Panzer Artillerie Regiment 3

4TH SS PANZERGRENADIER DIVISION *SS-POLIZEI*
SS-Panzergrenadier Regiment 7
SS-Panzergrenadier Regiment 8
SS-Artillerie Regiment 4
SS-Sturmgeschutz Abteilung 4

5TH SS PANZER DIVISION *WIKING*
SS-Panzergrenadier Regiment 9 *Germania*
SS-Panzergrenadier Regiment 10 *Westland*
SS-Panzer Regiment 5
SS-Panzer Artillerie Regiment 5

6TH SS GEBIRGS DIVISION *NORD*
SS-Gebirgsjäger Regiment 11 *Reinhard Heydrich*
SS-Gebirgsjäger Regiment 12 *Michael Gaissmair*
SS-Gebirgs Artillerie Regiment 6
SS-Sturmgeschutz Batterie 6

7TH SS FREIWILLIGEN-GEBIRGS DIVISION *PRINZ EUGEN*
SS-Freiwilligen Gebirgsjäger Regiment 13 *Artur Phleps*
SS-Freiwilligen Gebirgsjäger Regiment 14 *Skanderbeg*
SS-Freiwilligen Gebirgs Artillerie Regiment 7
SS-Sturmgeschutz Abteilung 7

8TH SS KAVALLERIE DIVISION *FLORIAN GEYER*
SS-Kavallerie Regiment 15
SS-Kavallerie Regiment 16
SS-Kavallerie Regiment 18
SS-Artillerie Regiment (mot) 8
SS-Panzerjäger Abteilung 8

9TH SS PANZER DIVISION *HOHENSTAUFEN*
SS-Panzergrenadier Regiment 19
SS-Panzergrenadier Regiment 20
SS-Panzer Regiment 9
SS-Panzer Artillerie Regiment 9

10TH SS PANZER DIVISION *FRUNDSBERG*
SS-Panzergrenadier Regiment 21
SS-Panzergrenadier Regiment 22
SS-Panzer Regiment 10
SS-Panzer Artillerie Regiment 10

11TH SS FREIWILLIGEN-PANZERGRENADIER DIVISION *NORDLAND*
SS-Panzergrenadier Regiment 23 *Norge*
SS-Panzergrenadier Regiment 24 *Danmark*
SS-Panzer Abteilung 11 *Hermann von Salza*
SS-Panzer Artillerie Regiment 11

12TH SS PANZER DIVISION *HITLERJUGEND*
SS-Panzergrenadier Regiment 25
SS-Panzergrenadier Regiment 26
SS-Panzer Regiment 12
SS-Panzer Artillerie Regiment 12

13TH WAFFEN-GEBIRGS DIVISION DER SS (KROATISCHE NR 1) *HANDSCHAR*
SS-Waffen Gebirgsjäger Regiment 27
SS-Waffen Gebirgsjäger Regiment 28
SS-Waffen Artillerie Regiment 13
SS-Panzerjäger Abteilung 13

14TH WAFFEN-GRENADIER DIVISION DER SS (UKRAINISCHE NR 1)
Waffen-Grenadier Regiment der SS 29
Waffen-Grenadier Regiment der SS 30
Waffen-Grenadier Regiment der SS 31
Waffen-Artillerie Regiment der SS 14

15TH WAFFEN-GRENADIER DIVISION DER SS (LETTISCHE NR 1)
Waffen-Grenadier Regiment der SS 32
Waffen-Grenadier Regiment der SS 33
Waffen-Grenadier Regiment der SS 34
Waffen-Artillerie Regiment der SS 15

16TH SS PANZERGRENADIER DIVISION *REICHSFÜHRER-SS*
SS-Panzergrenadier Regiment 35
SS-Panzergrenadier Regiment 36
SS-Artillerie Regiment 16
SS-Panzer Abteilung 16

17TH SS PANZERGRENADIER DIVISION *GÖTZ VON BERLICHINGEN*
SS-Panzergrenadier Regiment 37
SS-Panzergrenadier Regiment 38
SS-Panzer Artillerie Regiment 17
SS-Panzerjäger Abteilung 17

18TH SS FREIWILLIGEN-PANZERGRENADIER DIVISION *HORST WESSEL*
SS-Panzergrenadier Regiment 39
SS-Panzergrenadier Regiment 40
SS-Artillerie Regiment 18
SS-Panzerjäger Abteilung 18

**19TH WAFFEN-GRENADIER DIVISION DER SS
(LETTISCHES NR 2)**
Waffen-Grenadier Regiment der SS 42 Voldemars
Veiss
Waffen-Grenadier Regiment der SS 43 Heinrich
Schuldt
Waffen-Grenadier Regiment der SS 44
Waffen-Artillerie Regiment 19

**20TH WAFFEN-GRENADIER DIVISION DER SS
(ESTNISCHE NR 1)**
Waffen-Grenadier Division der SS 45
Waffen-Grenadier Division der SS 46
Waffen-Grenadier Division der SS 47
Waffen-Artillerie Regiment 20

**21ST WAFFEN-GEBIRGS DIVISION DER SS
(ALBANISCHE NR 1) *SKANDERBEG***
Waffen-Gebirgs Division der SS 50
Waffen-Gebirgs Division der SS 51
Waffen-Gebirgs Artillerie Regiment 21

**22ND FREIWILLIGEN-KAVALLREIE DIVISION DER SS
*MARIA THERESIA***
Freiwilligen-Kavallerie Regiment der SS 52
Freiwilligen-Kavallerie Regiment der SS 53
Freiwilligen-Kavallerie Regiment der SS 54
Freiwilligen-Kavallerie Regiment der SS 55

23RD WAFFEN-GEBIRGS DIVISION DER SS *KAMA*
Waffen-Gebirgsjäger Regiment der SS 56
Waffen-Gebirgsjäger Regiment der SS 57
Waffen-Gebirgsjäger Regiment der SS 58
Waffen-Gebirgs Artillerie Regiment der SS 23

**23RD FREIWILLIGEN-PANZERGRENADIER DIVISION
*NEDERLAND***
SS-Freiwilligen Panzergrenadier Regiment 48
General Seyffardt
SS-Freiwilligen Panzergrenadier Regiment 49 *De
Ruiter*

**24TH WAFFEN-GEBIRGS DIVISION DER SS
*KARSTJÄGER***
Waffen-Gebirgsjäger Regiment der SS 59
Waffen-Gebirgsjäger Regiment der SS 60
Waffen-Gebirgs Artillerie Regiment 24

**25TH WAFFEN-GRENADIERDIVISION DER SS
(UNGARISCHE NR 1) *HUNYADI***
Waffen-Grenadier Regiment der SS 61
Waffen-Grenadier Regiment der SS 62
Waffen-Grenadier Regiment der SS 63
Waffen-Artillerie Regiment der SS 25

**26TH WAFFEN-GRENADIER DIVISION DER SS
(UNGARISCHE NR 2) *HUNGARIA***
Waffen-Grenadier Regiment der SS 64
Waffen-Grenadier Regiment der SS 65
Waffen-Grenadier Regiment der SS 66
SS-Panzer Bataillon 26

**27TH SS FREIWILLIGEN-PANZERGRENADIER
DIVISION (FLÄMISCHE NR 1) *LANGEMARCK***

**28TH SS FREIWILLIGEN-PANZERGRENADIER
DIVISION *WALLONIEN***

**29TH WAFFEN-GRENADIER DIVISION DER SS
(RUSSISCHE NR 1)**

**29TH WAFFEN-GRENADIER DIVISION DER SS
(ITALIENISCHE NR 1)**
SS-Füsilier Bataillon *Debica*
SS-Füsilier Bataillon *Vendetta*

**30TH WAFFEN-GRENADIER DIVISION DER SS
(WEISSRUTHENISCHE NR 1)**
Waffen-Grenadier Regiment der SS 75
Waffen-Grenadier Regiment der SS 76
Waffen-Grenadier Regiment der SS 77
Waffen-Artillerie Regiment der SS 30

31ST SS-FREIWILLIGEN GRENADIER DIVISION
SS-Freiwilligen Grenadier Regiment 78
SS-Freiwilligen Grenadier Regiment 79
SS-Freiwilligen Grenadier Regiment 80
SS-Artillerie Regiment 31

**32ND SS FREIWILLIGEN GRENADIER DIVISION *30
JANUAR***

**33RD WAFFEN-KAVALLREIE DIVISION DER SS
(UNGARISCHE NR 3)**

**33RD WAFFEN-GRENADIER DIVISION DER SS
(FRANZÖSISCHE NR 1) *CHARLEMAGNE***

**34TH WAFFEN-GRENADIER DIVISION DER SS
*LANDSTORM NEDERLAND***
SS-Freiwilligen Grenadier Regiment 83
SS-Freiwilligen Grenadier Regiment 84

35TH SS POLIZEI GRENADIER DIVISION

36TH WAFFEN-GRENADIER DIVISION DER SS

**37TH SS FREIWILLIGEN-KAVALLREIE DIVISION
*LÜTZOW***

38th SS Grenadier Division *NIBELUNGEN*

Note: The theoretical strength of a Waffen-SS division was around 19,000 men, though those units
raised during the latter stages of the war never
approached this level of manpower. By the time
war ended in May 1945, the majority of the Waffen-
SS foreign volunteer units had been disbanded or
amalgamated with newly formed divisions in the
order of battle listed above. In addition to this list,
there were a number of minscule units which had
been raised by the SS, such as the Indian Legion.
However, these units were militarily useless.

COMMANDERS OF EUROPEAN UNITS AND EUROPEAN VOLUNTEERS DECORATED WITH THE KNIGHT'S CROSS OF THE IRON CROSS ON THE EASTERN FRONT

The dates listed indicate the time of the award of the Knight's Cross. Where applicable, awards for higher degrees of the Knight's Cross – Oakleaves, Oakleaves with Swords, and Diamonds – are also listed, with the specific award in brackets, together with the recipient's position in the league table pertaining to the award of that specific higher classification of the Knight's Cross. Ranks of recipients are also given.

III (Germanic) SS Panzer Corps

Steiner, Felix
10.8.44 (Swords, 86th)
SS-Obergruppenführer
und General der Waffen-SS
23.12.1942 (Oakleaves, 159th)
15.8.1940 (Knight's Cross)

V SS Mountain Corps

Phleps, Artur
24.11.44 (Oakleaves, 670th)
SS-Obergruppenführer
und General der Waffen-SS
4.7.43 (Knight's Cross of the Iron Cross)

VI Waffen Army Corps of the SS (Latvian)

Krueger, Walter
1.2.45 (Swords, 120th)
SS-Obergruppenführer
and General of the Waffen-SS
31.8.43 (Oakleaves, 286th)
13.12.1941 (Knight's Cross of the Iron Cross)

IX Waffen Mountain Corps of the SS (Croatian)

Pfeffer-Wildenbruch, Karl
4.2.45 (Oakleaves, 723rd)
SS-Obergruppenführer
and General of the Waffen-SS
11.1.45 (Knight's Cross of the Iron Cross)

Corps Pioneer Commander III (Germanic) SS Panzer Corps

Schaefer, Max
25.1.45 (Oakleaves, 714th)
SS-Standartenführer
22.2.43 (Knight's Cross of the Iron Cross)

7th SS Freiwilligen-Gebirgs Division *Prinz Eugen*

Dietsche, Bernhard
17.7.43 SS-Sturmbannführer

Krombholz, Franz
28.3.45 SS-Hauptsturmführer

Kumm, Otto
4.4.45 (Swords, 138th)
SS-Brigadeführer and Major-General of the Waffen-SS
6.4.43 (Knight's Cross of the Iron Cross)

Neumann, Eggert
3.11.44 SS-Sturmbannführer

Paletta, Harry
26.11.44
SS-Obersturmbannführer

Petersen, Heinrich
13.11.43
SS-Obersturmbannführer

11th SS Freiwilligen-Panzergrenadier Division *Nordland*

Bunse, Fritz
30.1.44 SS-Sturmbannführer

Christophersen, Egon
11.7.44 SS-Unterscharführer

Fischer, Alred
9.5.45 SS-Sturmbannführer

Gieseler, Karl-Heinz
29.4.45
SS-Obersturmbannführer

Guerz, Martin
23.10.44 SS-Hauptsturmführer

Haemel, Heinz
16.6.44 SS-Hauptsturmführer

Hektor, Albert
23.8.44 SS-Oberscharführer

Hund, Willi
20.4.45 SS-Obersturmführer

Kam, Soeren
7.2.45 SS-Untersturmführer

Karl, Friedrich-Wilhelm
26.12.44
SS-Obersturmbannführer

Kausch, Paul-Albert
23.8.44
SS-Obersturmbannführer

Knöchlein, Fritz
16.11.44
SS-Obersturmbannführer

Kruegel, Albrecht
12.3.44 SS-Sturmbannführer

Langendorf, Georg
12.3.44 SS-Untersturmführer

Luengen, Siegfried
16.11.44 SS-Hauptscharführer

Potschka, Herman
26.12.44 SS-Sturmbannführer

Rott, Rudolf
28.2.45 SS-Obersturmführer

Saalbach, Rudolf
12.3.44 SS-Hauptsturmführer

Scholz, Fritz
SS-Gruppenführer and Lieutenant-General of the Waffen-SS
8.8.44 (Swords, 85th)
12.3.44 (Oakleaves, 423rd)
18.1.42 (Knight's Cross of the Iron Cross)

Seebach, Walter
12.3.44 SS-Obersturmführer

Sporck, Kaspar
23.10.44 SS-Unterschführer

Spoerle, Richard
16.11.44 SS-Hauptsturmführer

Schulz-Streeck, Karl-Heinz
2.5.45 SS-Sturmbannführer

Stoffers, Arnold
12.3.44
SS-Obersturmbannführer

Vogt, Fritz
16.3.45 (Oakleaves, 785th)
SS-Hauptsturmführer
4. 9.44 (Knight's Cross of the Iron Cross)

Wild, Philipp
21.3.44 SS-Oberscharführer

Ziegler, Joachim
28.4.45 (Oakleaves, 848th)
SS-Brigadeführer

13th Waffen-Gebirgs Division der SS *Handschar*

Hampel, Desiderius
3.5.45 SS-Standartenführer

Kinz, Hemlut
3.5.45 SS-Hauptsturmführer

Liecke, Karl
3.5.45 SS-Sturmbannführer
and Major of the Police

Stenwedel, Albert
3.5.45 SS-Sturmbannführer

14th Waffen-Grenadier Division der SS

Freitag, Fritz
30.9.44 SS-Brigadeführer and Major-General of the Waffen-SS

15th Waffen-Grenadier Division der SS

Aperats, Karlis	21.9.44 SS-Obersturmbannführer
Ax, Adolf	9.5.45 SS-Oberführer
Heilmann, Nikolaus	13.8.44 SS-Oberführer
Sensberg, Karlis	9.5.44 SS-Unterscharführer

19th Waffen-Grenadier Division der SS

Adamsons, Mervaldis	25.4.34 SS-Untersturmführer
Ancans, Robert	25.1.45 SS-Untersturmführer
Ansons, Zanis	25.1.45 SS-Hauptscharführer
Butkus, Zanis	21.9.44 SS-Hauptsturmführer
Gaigals, Roberts	5.5.45 SS-Obersturmführer
Galdins, Nikolajs	25.1.45 SS-Obersturmbannführer
Reinholds, Voldemar	9.5.45 SS-Sturmbannführer
Riekstins, Alfreds	5.4.45 SS-Unterscharführer
Schuldt, Hinrich	25.3.44 (Swords, 56th) SS-Brigadeführer and Major-General of the Waffen-SS ? 4 43 (Oakleaves, 220th) 5 4 42 (Knight's Cross of the Iron Cross)
Streckenbach, Bruno	21.1.45 (Oakleaves, 701st) SS-Gruppenführer and Lieutenant-General of the Police 27.8.44 (Knight's Cross of the Iron Cross)
Veiss, Voldemars	9.2.44 SS-Standartenführer

20th Waffen-Grenadier Division der SS

Augsberger, Franz	31.3.45 SS-Brigadeführer and Major-General of the Waffen-SS
Langhorst, Bernhard	5.4.45 SS-Sturmbannführer
Maitla, Paul	23.8.44 SS-Hauptsturmführer
Nugiseks, Harald	9. 4.44 SS-Unterscharführer
Rebane, Alfons	9.5.45 (Oakleaves, 875th) SS-Standartenführer 23.2.44 (Knight's Cross of the Iron Cross)
Riipalu, Harald	23.8.44 SS-Obersturmbannführer

SS Volunteer Panzegrenadier Battalion *Narwa*, 5th SS Panzer Division *Wiking*

Eberhardt, Georg	4.8.43 SS-Sturmbannführer

22nd SS Freiwilligen-Kavallerie Division der SS *Maria Theresia*

Ameiser, Anton	1.11.44 SS-Sturmbannführer
Vandieken, Anton	26.12.44 SS-Hauptsturmführer
Zehender, August	4.2.45 (Oakleaves, 722nd) SS-Brigadeführer and Major-General of the Waffen-SS

SS Volunteer Legion *Nederland*

Mooyman, Gerardes	20.2.43 SS-Sturmmann

23rd SS Freiwilligen-Panzergrenadier Division *Nederland*

Behler, Clemens	17.3.45 SS-Obersturmführer
Bruins, Derk-Elsko	23.8.44 SS-Rottenführer
Collani, Hans	19.8.44 SS-Obersturmbannführer
Ertel, Karl-Heinz	23.8.44 SS-Hauptsturmführer
Frühauf, Carl-Heinz	4.6.44 SS-Hauptsturmführer
Hellmers, Johannes	5.3.45 SS-Obersturmführer
Hofer, Lothar	5.4.45 SS-Sturmbannführer and Major of the Police
Jenschke, Walter	18.12.44 Gunner
Joerchel, Wolfgang	21.4.44 SS-Obersturmbannführer
Lohmann, Hanns-Heinrich	9.5.45 (Oakleaves, 872nd) SS-Obersturmbannführer 12.3.44 (Knight's Cross of the Iron Cross)
Meyer, Hans	2.9.44 SS-Hauptsturmführer
Petersen, Otto	11.12.44 SS-Hauptsturmführer
Ruehle, von Lilienstern Hans J.	2.2.44 SS-Hauptsturmführer
Rieth, Herbert-Albert	11.12.44 SS-Untersturmführer
Scheibe, Siegfried	9.5.45 SS-Sturmbannführer
Schlueter, Wilhelm	23.8.44 SS-Sturmbannführer and Major of the Police
Schluifelder, Georg	26.11.44 SS-Standartenoberjunker
Scholz, Helmut	24.9.44 (Oakleaves, 591st) SS-Obersturmführer 4.6.44 (Knight's Cross of the Iron Cross)
Strapatin, Stefan	16.11.44 SS-Rottenführer
Wanhoefer, Günter	27.8.44 SS-Hauptsturmführer
Wagner, Jürgen	29.12.44 (Oakleaves, 680th) SS-Brigadeführer and Major-General of the Waffen-SS 24.7.43 Knight's Cross of the Iron Cross)

27th SS Freiwilligen-Panzergrenadier Division *Langemarck*

Schellong, Conrad	28.2.45 SS-Sturmbannführer
Schrynen, Remi	21.9.44 SS-Sturmmann

28th SS Freiwilligen-Panzergrenadier Division *Wallonien*

Degrelle, Léon	27.8.44 SS-Sturmbannführer (Oakleaves) 20.2.44 (Knight's Cross of the Iron Cross)
Gillis, Leon	30.9.44 SS-Untersturmführer
Leroy, Jaques	20.4.45 SS-Untersturmführer

33rd Waffen-Grenadier Division der SS *Charlemagne*

Fenet, Henri-Joseph	29.4.45 SS-Hauptsturmführer
Vaulot, Eugène	29.4.45 SS-Unterscharführer

WAFFEN-SS RANKS AND THEIR ENGLISH EQUIVALENTS

SS-Schüte	Private
SS-Oberschütze	Senior Private, attained after six months' service
SS-Sturmmann	Lance-Corporal
SS-Rottenführer	Corporal
SS-Unterscharführer	Senior Corporal/ Lance-Sergeant
SS-Scharführer	Sergeant
SS-Oberscharführer	Staff Sergeant
SS-Hauptscharführer	Warrant Officer
SS-Sturmscharführer	Senior Warrant Officer after 15 years' service
SS-Untersturmführer	Second Lieutenant
SS-Obersturmführer	First Lieutenant
SS-Hauptsturmführer	Captain
SS-Sturmbannführer	Major
SS-Oberbannsturmführer	Lieutenant-Colonel
SS-Standartenführer	Colonel
SS-Oberführer	Senior Colonel
SS-Brigadeführer und Generalmajor der Waffen-SS	Major-General
SS-Gruppenführer und Generalleutnant der Waffen-SS	Lieutenant-General
SS-Obergruppenführer und General der Waffen-SS	General
SS-Oberstgruppenführer und Generaloberst der Waffen-SS	Colonel-General
Reichsführer-SS	(no English equivalent)

WAFFEN-SS RANKS OF OFFICER CANDIDATES

Early 1940	SS-Junker
	SS-Standartenjunker
	SS-Standartenoberjunker
From July 1943	Führer-Bewerber
	SS-Junker
	SS-Standartenjunker
	SS-Standartenoberjunker

WAFFEN-SS RANKS OF NCO CANDIDATES

SS-Unterführer-Anwärter Signed for 12 years' service
SS-Unterführer-Bewerber Signed for less than 12 years' service

Titles of lower ranks were affected by the type of unit the soldier was assigned to. Also, in two further special circumstances the prefix 'SS' before the rank title was substituted by the word 'Legion', abbreviated to 'Leg.' or 'Waffen'. Rank titles for men serving in foreign legions were amended to Leg.-Schütze, Leg.-Sturmman and so on. Divisions made up primarily of non-Germanic volunteers or conscripts, designated 'Waffen-SS Division der SS', had their rank title changed, i.e. Waffen-Oberbannsturmführer der SS, Waffen-Standartenführer der SS. The following table is a list of the rank titles for privates and senior privates in specific types of unit. The first column is the unit type, the second the title of a private in that unit and the third the title of a senior private in that unit. The title for ranks above senior private are given on the page opposite.

SS-Panzer-Regiment	SS-Panzerschütze	SS-Panzeroberschütze
SS-Panzergrenadier Regiment	SS-Panzergrenadier	SS-Panzerobergrenadier
SS-Grenadier Regiment	SS-Grenadier	SS-Obergrenadier
SS-Gebirgs-Jäger-Regiment	SS-Jäger	SS-Oberschütze
SS-Reiter-Regiment	SS-Reiter	SS-Oberreiter
SS-Artillery-Regiment	SS-Kanonier	SS-Oberkanonier
SS-Gebirgs-Artillery-Regiment	SS-Kanonier	SS-Oberkanonier
SS-Sturmgesch.-Einheit	SS-Kanonier	SS-Oberkanonier
SS-Panzer-Jäger-Einheit	SS-Schütze	SS-Oberschütze
SS-Kradschutzen.-Einheit	SS-Schütze	SS-Oberschütze
SS-Panzer-Späh.-Einheit	SS-Panzerschütze	SS-Panzeroberschutze
SS-Flak-Einheit	SS-Kanonier	SS-Oberkanonier
SS-Pionier-Einheit	SS-Pionier	SS-Oberpionier
SS-Nachrichten-Einheit	SS-Funker	SS-Obefunker
SS-Werfer-Einheit	SS-Kanonier	SS-Oberkanonier
SS-Radfahr-Einheit	SS-Schütze	SS-Oberschütze
SS-Nachschub-Einheit (Besp.)	SS-Fahrer	SS-Oberfahrer
SS-Nachschub-Einheit (Mot.)	SS-Kraftfahrer	SS-Oberkraftfahrer
SS-Sanitäts-Einheit	SS-Schütze	SS-Oberschütze
SS-Veterinär-Einheit	SS-Reiter	SS-Oberreiter
SS-Werkstatt-Einheit	SS-Schütze	SS-Oberschütze
SS-Feldgend.-Einheit	SS-Feldgendarm	
SS-Karstwehr-Bataillon	SS-Jäger	SS-Oberschütze
SS-Wehrgeologen-Bataillon	SS-Schütze	SS-Oberschütze
SS-Kriegsberichter Abteilung	SS-Schütze	SS-Oberschütze
SS-Jäger-Bataillon 502	SS-Bewährungsschütze	

INDEX